SUCCESSFUL WRITING

PUBLISHING A BOOK

How to publish your own work
and make a profit

Robert Spicer

3rd edition

How To Books

Cartoons by Mike Flanagan

British Library Cataloguing-in-publication data
A catalogue record for this book is available from the British Library.

Copyright © 1998 by Robert Spicer

Published by How To Books, 3 Newtec Place, Magdalen Road,
Oxford OX4 1RE, United Kingdom. Tel: (01865) 793806.
Fax: (01865) 248780.

First edition 1993
Second edition 1995
Third edition (revised) 1998

Note: The material contained in this book is set out in good faith for
general guidance and no liability can be accepted for loss or expense
incurred as a result of relying in particular circumstances on statements
made in the book. The laws and regulations are complex and liable to
change, and readers should check the current position with the relevant
authorities before making personal arrangements.

Produced for How To Books by Deer Park Productions.
Typeset by Concept Communications Ltd, Crayford, Kent.
Printed and bound by The Cromwell Press, Trowbridge, Wiltshire.

Preface

to Third Edition

It has never been easier to publish your own book. If you have some cash, and access to a computer, you can produce attractively designed and competitively priced books with comparative ease. This, the creative part of publishing, is well within the reach of most people who can read and write. There is nothing magical or secret about the publishing industry. Many of its techniques are explained in the first part of this book.

But the difficult parts of publishing – distribution, marketing and sales – are not so easily learned. It is not easy to sell books. To put the problem at its most basic: why should anyone buy your book instead of five or six pints of beer? If you can answer this question positively, and have the drive and determination to carry your marketing plans through, then you can become, in financial terms, a successful publisher.

For those who have received many rejection slips from publishers, take heart! In fairness, your work may have been turned down because it is simply unpublishable or of very poor quality, but remember that many successful and well-respected literary figures have found it extremely difficult to get their work into print.

Two prominent examples of this are Jack London and Samuel Beckett. Beckett sent books to publishers for twenty years, with very limited success. It was only when his play *Waiting for Godot* was staged successfully in France that publishers fought to handle his work. He is now recognised as one of the leading authors of the twentieth century.

If you really believe in the value of your work, and you cannot persuade the big publishing corporations to take it on, then hopefully this book will help you to do it yourself without risking large amounts of money.

Readers are advised to seek expert professional advice before making important business, legal or financial decisions, and this book must not be considered a substitute for such advice.

This third edition has been revised and updated to take account of developments in the publishing industry in recent years. Legal developments have also been included.

Many people have helped during the preparation of this book. I would like to thank How To Books for their invaluable advice, encouragement and assistance. I would also like to acknowledge permission to reproduce copyright material, given by the Public Lending Right Office, Mr A. T. Smail, J. Whitaker & Sons Ltd. and the Publishing Training Centre at Book House.

Robert Spicer

Contents

List of Illustrations

9

1
Getting Started

This chapter deals with the following:

- what is the aim of do-it-yourself publishing?
- selling and distribution
- publishing in Britain today
- vanity publishing
- clarifying your aims
- cash problems
- the practical requirements of independent publishing
- the advantages of specialising.

But first let's see how two would-be publishers might approach the task.

A TALE OF TWO PUBLISHERS

1. A success story. Breakeven Publishing: how to publish your book *and* get your money back

Harry Bright had always wanted to write a book about life in his town during World War Two. His brother ran a bookshop and he encouraged Harry to write and publish his book. Harry wrote the book in longhand. His brother typed it into his word processor. They then contacted six different local printers for quotes on the cost of producing the book. Eventually, they chose a community printing co-operative which was prepared to give a large discount for cash payment, half on delivery of the book and half on completion of the job.

Harry's brother knew a young graphic design student who took on the design work in his own time. While the designer and the printer were at work, Harry and his brother sent out circulars to all their friends and relations, to local radio and newspapers, libraries, museums and organisations telling them about the book.

In October, on the fiftieth anniversary of the bombing of the town, the book was published. Harry was interviewed by the local newspaper and on the radio. By Christmas, he had sold all 1,000 copies of his book, at £9.99 each. After paying the printer and the designer and informing the Inland Revenue of his income, he took a long holiday in the South of France to write his next book.

2. A cautionary tale: how not to publish your book

Arthur Bloggs was a keen amateur photographer. He had taken a large number of pictures of railway locomotives. A friend suggested to him that they would make a good book. Arthur managed to persuade the friend to give him financial backing to publish the photographs in book form.

Arthur contacted a printer at random from *Yellow Pages*. He chose the best quality paper, a large size format and the finest methods of photographic reproduction, regardless of expense. He borrowed £500 from his friend to pay a deposit to the printer.

Ten thousand copies of *Arthur Bloggs' Railway Locomotives* were printed, priced at £11.99 each. Arthur had no room in his house to store them, so he arranged for them to be kept in a friend's garage. He did not know that the garage roof was leaking.

Publication day was January 2. Arthur threw a champagne party for the press but no-one came. He advertised his book in railway magazines and national newspapers. He gave away 200 copies to friends and relations who promised to pay but never did. He kept no record of these copies.

Arthur signed a contract with a national distribution firm to distribute 500 copies of the book. After a year, only 200 copies had been sold. The company pulped the remainder. The other 4,800 copies languished in his friend's garage, getting ever more mouldy, until eventually they were thrown onto a skip.

Arthur was made bankrupt when he could not pay the printer's bill. He had to sell his house and now lives in a bedsit.

The story of Arthur Bloggs is a true one. Only the names have been changed to protect the innocent.

It illustrates very clearly how things can go wrong if you get carried away with the idea of publishing your own book and do not apply strict controls. On the other hand, you should remember that it is not only amateur publishers who can come unstuck. Most commercial publishing firms, if they chose, could tell horror stories about books which have lost large amounts of money, disappearing manuscripts, missing pages and covers stuck on upside down.

AIMS OF THIS BOOK

One aim of this book is to help would-be publishers to avoid the problems encountered by Arthur Bloggs. The methods set out below are those which we used for our own publishing. We do not say they are the only methods, or the best ones, or those used by commercial publishing firms, but we do think that if the following principles are applied, with an element of luck, you can publish your own book efficiently, with every chance of getting it out to a good number of readers and at least breaking even in financial terms. Realistically, we do not think that the amateur publisher should usually hope for much more.

The most difficult problems facing amateur publishers are marketing and distribution. Given enough cash, anyone can get a book printed but not everyone can get it into the hands of paying customers. This book therefore contains essential detail on the sales side of publishing in the hope of advising would-be publishers on how to sell, and so avoid ending up with a warehouse of unsold and unsaleable books.

It is relatively easy to write a sound book but it is very difficult to get it commercially published. This is surprising when you see the poor quality of some of the material in bookshops. In 1998 many of the best selling books in Britain are TV and film spinoffs or material produced by 'celebrities'. If your name is not known and you have no contacts in the media world, you have very little chance of having your work accepted by a commercial publisher. So if you have written, or are going to write, a book which you consider worth publication you may well find that it is disappointingly rejected by established publishing firms, most of whom are inundated all the time with new publishing proposals.

To overcome such disappointment this book sets out to show how you can do it yourself. It does not go into too much detail about the technicalities of printing processes, except to give a basic overview. In our view, printing is best left to a professional printer. The most relevant technical printing terms are explained in the glossary, and a selection of books on the subject is included in the section on further reading.

CLARIFYING YOUR AIMS

Vanity publishing

Publishing your own book can be a worthwhile exercise, very interesting and even exciting at times and to see your writing in book form with your name on the cover can be most pleasing.

This sometimes causes people to pay to have their book published by what are known as 'vanity' or 'subsidy' publishers, many of whom advertise in the Sunday press and in magazines. As the name implies, the book is only being published to satisfy the ego of the writer irrespective of the quality of the work — and this is extremely expensive (several thousands of pounds). Vanity publishing means paying someone else to do the whole job. The conventional wisdom is: don't do it!

The drawbacks of vanity publishing

● Remember that vanity publishers will usually print an agreed number of copies in 'sheet' form but will only actually bind a few copies.

● Book reviewers in newspapers know who the vanity publishers are and they won't generally review their books. (They won't usually review the work of a small publisher either.)

● Bookshops won't normally stock vanity published books.

● Never pay for publication. If a book really is worth issuing on sale to the general public it should sell enough to cover costs.

Your motives for publishing

Before you start making financial decisions it is worth examining your motives. For example:

● Vanity — eg to see your name in print?

● To promote a cause — eg to publicise the plight of endangered wildlife?

● For fund-raising — eg any profit from publishing to go to charity?

● To make money — eg for yourself or an organisation?

● To provide information as a service — eg publishing a 'Members Handbook'?

● In association with, for example, a company, school or university or other institution — eg to mark a centenary?

● The pure pleasure of self-publishing — learning to handle words, design and print?

If you are frustrated from receiving standard rejection slips from commercial publishers, remember that this does not mean that your book is bad (although it may well be!). It simply means that the publishers have decided that the subject matter is wrong for their list, or that they cannot sell it in commercial quantities.

THE PRACTICAL REQUIREMENTS OF INDEPENDENT PUBLISHING

Cash

The first thing you will need is a certain amount of money to pay the bills as you go along. This will probably be £3,000 to £4,000 for the type of paperback you are now reading, though an exact figure would depend on the type of book and quantity to be printed. One of the objectives of this book is to show you how to keep down the cost of production. Another is to show how to maximise the sales of your book in order to cover your costs.

If you cannot afford any financial risk at all, stop now — but remember that one aim of this book is to show how to reduce the financial risk to an absolute minimum. If you follow the principles set out, the worst that you could lose would be the cost of, say, a Caribbean cruise. At the end of the cruise you would have a beautiful tan and several rolls of film. How would this compare with having your own book in print?

Amateur publishers need to be aware of any and all possibilities for saving and making cash. Could your book be an attractive prospect for advertisers to insert their own material? This could be a distinct possibility in the case of local interest or specialised books. You could telephone or visit local traders, or even contact the marketing departments of national firms, to see if they would be interested. One important factor in selling advertising space is the likely make-up of your readership, so make sure that you tell potential advertisers exactly what kind of people the book is aimed at.

On the other hand, you could equal the achievement of Aeron Clement whose book on badgers, *The Cold Moons*, sold 8,000 copies when privately published. It was subsequently published by Penguin and has sold over 100,000 copies. It is also worth remembering that Beatrix Potter published her own first book after rejection by commercial publishers. But these were very exceptional cases.

Time and energy

You will in effect be running a small business with all the time-consuming

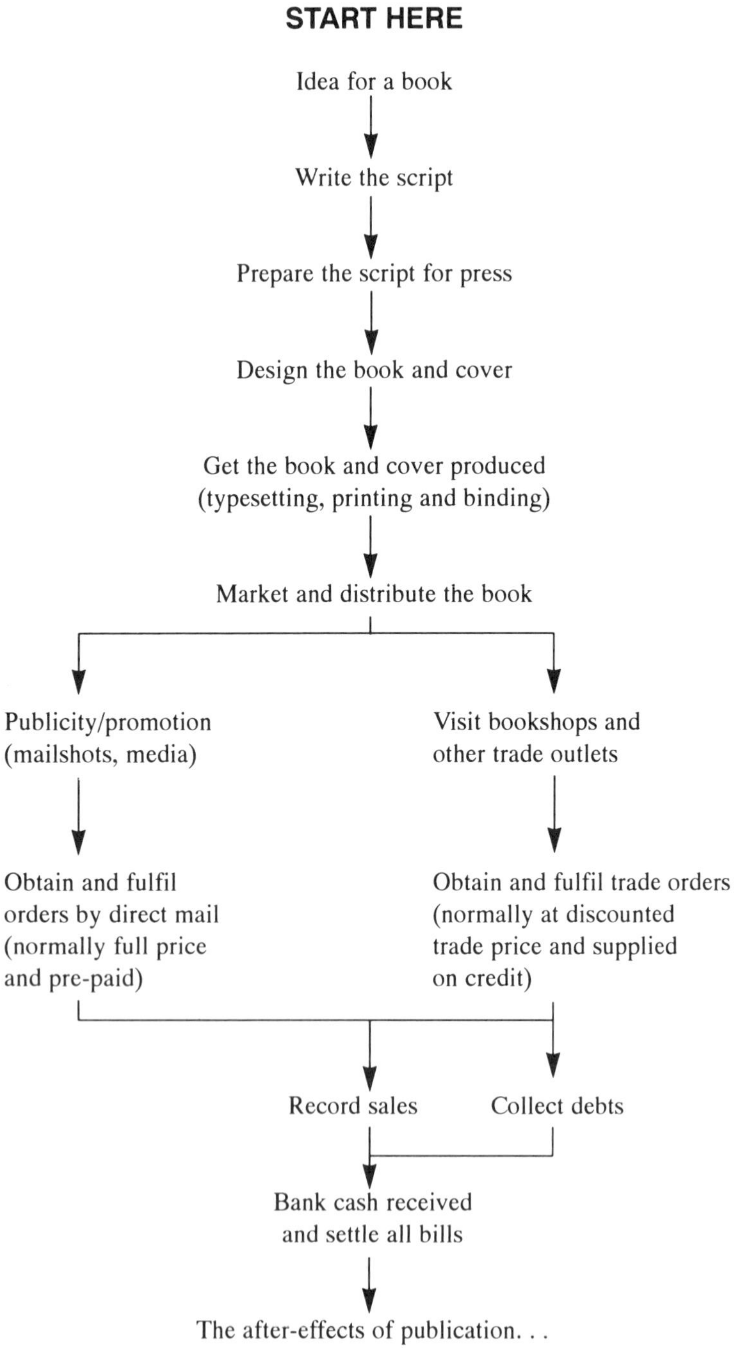

START HERE

Idea for a book

↓

Write the script

↓

Prepare the script for press

↓

Design the book and cover

↓

Get the book and cover produced
(typesetting, printing and binding)

↓

Market and distribute the book

Publicity/promotion
(mailshots, media)

↓

Obtain and fulfil
orders by direct mail
(normally full price
and pre-paid)

Visit bookshops and
other trade outlets

↓

Obtain and fulfil trade orders
(normally at discounted
trade price and supplied
on credit)

Record sales   Collect debts

↓

Bank cash received
and settle all bills

↓

The after-effects of publication. . .

Fig. 1. A simple flowchart of the publishing process.

and energy-sapping jobs which this involves, but the excitement and potential rewards can certainly compensate for this. Many of the points made in this book would apply to businesses in general, not only to book publishing.

Business and management sense

You must be able to manage your time and resources in the most efficient way possible. This may cause problems if you have never run your own business before. Remember, there are no monthly salary cheques in the self-publishing game. This book aims to help you to become an efficient manager of your own enterprise.

Luck

We are not able to help with this essential element! Management consultants are increasingly aware of the importance of luck and are trying to analyse and advise on this element. Random chance, good fortune, being in the right place at the right time — these are intangible ideas. Everyone is lucky at some time in their lives but the successful business person learns to recognise good portents and to take advantage of them. The importance of luck should be better recognised and prepared for, so that opportunities can be seized when they arise.

THE ADVANTAGE OF SPECIALISING

It is fair to say that you will have a much greater chance of success (defined in our limited terms as getting a book out for sale to readers while not losing large amounts of cash) if you produce a book in a specialist niche area. For example, it is almost impossible to successfully publish a work of fiction by an unknown author. Even established publishers have the greatest difficulties with that. Nonfiction books of local or specialised interest are far more likely to succeed, if they are of good quality, and genuinely relate to readers' own interests, not just your own. You will also find it much easier to get reviews in specialist magazines rather than in the mass media.

GETTING EXPERT HELP

To improve your own chances of publishing success, try to make use of experts in their respective fields. Also in the 'How To' series there are books to help you on your way, such as:

Copyright & Law for Writers (Helen Shay)
How to Do Your Own Advertising (Michael Bennie)
How to Do Your Own P.R. (Ian Phillipson)
How to Start a Business from Home (Graham Jones)
Making Money from Writing (Carole Baldock)
Managing Your Business Accounts (Peter Taylor)
Successful Mail Order Marketing (Ian Bruce)
Writing & Publishing Poetry (Stephen Wade)
Writing & Selling a Novel (Marina Oliver)
Writing a Non-fiction Book (Norman Toulson)
Writing for Publication (Chriss McCallum)

CHECKLIST

1. Have you decided why you want to publish a book?

2. Do you have enough cash available to get you started?

3. Are you prepared to devote your spare time and energy to publishing your book?

FINAL COMMENT

If the book which you want to publish is a work of fiction, don't be discouraged. Although selling novels is more difficult than selling 'niche' books, you can succeed. Remember Jack London and Samuel Beckett!

2
Preparing the Raw Material

It is said that everyone has a book inside them, either fact or fiction, which is crying out to be written. You do not need to be a literary genius. There are very few Charles Dickens or even Jeffrey Archers in the world, so cast off your inhibitions and have a go!

Most fictional tales are based on personal experiences or reminiscences. Practical books can offer a wealth of experience and advice. If you have persevered and produced a manuscript, don't push it into a closet but set about having it published.

This chapter deals with the following:

● how to prepare the script

● knowing the limits to freedom of expression.

PREPARING A SCRIPT FOR PUBLICATION

Handwriting

This is for many people the most pleasant way to write a book, sitting by the fire in the winter or in the garden during fine weather. Any additions can be easily made. On completion, however, the work has to be converted into typeset material ('camera ready copy') for the printers, and typesetting can be expensive. Make sure your writing is readable, otherwise you will encounter all kinds of problems and unexpected costs. You might be charged more for typesetting from handwritten material, than if it were typed. Check this out; it may pay you to have your script typed before sending it to the typesetter or printer.

Typing

Again the finished typed material has to be typeset. Make sure that your typing is clear and then where there are many alterations retype it. Use A4 size paper, and make all the typing double spaced lines, with generous margins left and right.

Word-processing the script

Books can be written directly on a word processor. They can also be converted from handwriting and typing into material which needs less typesetting and so keeps costs down. Unless you have a definite need for it there is no need to go to the expense of purchasing a word processor as one can be hired, leased or borrowed instead. In *Yellow Pages* you will find a large number of advertisements about local word processor services, some of which offer tuition if required. Local newspapers also carry advertisements to the same end and it would be worthwhile checking for quotations on the cost of converting your books.

                                    BREAKEVEN PUBLISHING
                                    June 199X

Dear Sir/Madam

I am writing to you to ask whether you could let me have an estimate for typing or word-processing the manuscript of a book which I have written, and for providing me with two copies, double-spaced, on A4 paper.

The manuscript consists of 250 pages of handwritten script, and amounts to 85,000 words approximately.

Could you please let me know the length of time which it would take to convert this material into typescript? A sample page is enclosed.

Yours sincerely

Harry Bright

Fig. 2. Enquiring about the cost of typing or word-processing a manuscript.

The word processor should be used to produce copy that cuts down the work of the typesetter, notably in these ways:

- justification
- indents
- editing
- storing text on disk.

Justification
This means that both the left and right hand sides of the pages of the book are straight and parallel. A word processor can be set up to do this automatically. Text not justified, for example on the right hand side, is said to be 'unjustified right' or 'ragged right'.

Indents
These occur where words are set in from the margin, normally to start a paragraph. There are many examples of indents in the book which you are now reading. The normal indent is one em, a printer's measurement meaning one sixth of an inch.

Editing
A paragraph may end with a line consisting of just a few words on another page (a 'widow line'). The poor appearance of this can be adjusted easily on a word processor by removing an unnecessary word or words from the page. On resetting the word processor will readjust the whole page.

Disk
The finished article from the word processor can be stored on a 'disk', a small cassette-like object, which the typesetter will use to produce the typesetting electronically rather than manually. Check that the one you are producing is 'compatible' for use by the typesetter you have chosen.

Can't everything be done on a computer?
If you are a computer expert, or have your own machine, you will know the power of computers to cut out stages in publishing a book. Computer programs are now available which include spelling checkers, grammar and style checkers and word counters. Programs are also produced which contain a database of 5,000 plots and characters which can be used to create an infinite number of stories.

It is also possible for computers to read handwriting and convert it into electronic data. Indeed, computers have now become so sophisticated that they are able, through voice recognition, to convert the spoken word in the same way. It is thus conceivable that you could dictate a book into one end of a machine and thousands of copies of a complete book would come out of the other, rather like a literary combine harvester. This is no longer pure science fiction.

However, we would advise that a computer be treated as a tool like any other. If you really want to spend eight hours a day in front of a computer screen, instead of working with paper and ink, then you should note the following:

Guidance on using a computer

- The rush of businesses to computerise has started to rebound. It is now emerging that employees who spend long periods of time working at computer keyboards can develop serious illnesses. These can include RSI (repetitive strain injury) and eye problems. Employers have already had to pay out large sums in compensation for such injuries. A recent case involved two British Telecom employees who were awarded £6,000 damages as compensation for repetitive strain injury caused by keyboard work at high speed, using inappropriate furniture. British Telecom appealed against the judgment but the matter was settled out of court on undisclosed terms, and the appeal effectively abandoned. This case is not a binding precedent but it was the first of its type to come to court.

- More recently, in the case of *Pickford v ICI Ltd* (1996), a secretary employed by ICI had spent three-quarters of each of her eight-hour working days typing. She developed writer's cramp and claimed compensation from ICI. The Court of Appeal allowed her claim and stated that it was plainly foreseeable that typists might contract writer's cramp if they typed for prolonged periods without a break. It has recently been estimated that 5 million working days are lost each year because of upper limb disorders caused by keyboard work. Schoolchildren are reportedly beginning to suffer. One environmentally sound solution is to keep a goose in the back garden for a good supply of quills!

- The best advice to employers and computer users generally is: use computers and don't let them use you. Also note that salespersons dealing with computer software and hardware will never mention the possible medical effects of long-term use. In a *Financial Times* article, Stanley Kalms, boss of Dixons for 44 years, stated that he preferred pen and ink to computer technology and that he could not use a computer. If he has managed to run 800 high-technology information shops so successfully without using a computer then you can be confident of publishing your own book without one!

● What about desktop publishing? This is a general term for computer programs which can arrange combinations of text and pictures in any number of sophisticated ways. These programs are good for small in-house runs but useless for long print runs unless you have a very expensive printer. Some users make the claim that the availability of cheap desktop publishing systems will revolutionise publishing. We remain sceptical of such claims, except for the production of souped-up pamphlets. The health problems caused by long hours spent before computer screens and keyboards, which are only now starting to emerge, never seem to be taken into account by desktop publishing enthusiasts.

● Personal computers and word processors have continued to develop apace since the last edition of this book. From the do-it-yourself publisher's point of view, the following developments are significant:

– Colour printers are now very cheap. They give self-publishers wide scope for experimentation with the arrangement of words and pictures.

– The Internet is now within the reach of anyone with an up-to-date personal computer. This is a global system of connections between computers through telephone lines. John Updike has recently published the first chapter of a novel on the Internet and has invited contributions to further chapters. Publishing on the Internet is at present in its infancy. Further developments must be expected.

THE LIMITS TO FREEDOM OF EXPRESSION

What are you going to write about? Be careful because there are restrictions on freedom of expression. These cover:

● copyright

● libel

● contempt of court

● obscenity

● blasphemy

- privacy and confidentiality

- racial hatred

- official secrets.

Some of these topics are legal minefields. This book cannot hope to cover all the legal technicalities in detail. It can give general guidance on problem areas to be avoided. If in doubt, see a lawyer. However, remember that even a short and simple piece of advice from a solicitor can be very expensive. You might be able to keep legal costs down by approaching Citizens' Advice Bureaux or advice centres, or even by doing your own legal research, but extreme caution must be your watchword. Let's consider them each in turn.

Copyright

The law forbids using other people's written words without their consent. Copyright protection covers, in general, the author of words, not the creator of ideas. A person whose copyright is infringed can get a court order preventing further breach and financial compensation. Breach of copyright is the professional publisher's nightmare and general guidance can only be:

DO NOT COPY OTHER PEOPLE'S WORK
WITHOUT THEIR PERMISSION

For example, in a recent case where magazine publishers reproduced copies of advertisements which had appeared in another magazine, the court stated that they were liable for breach of copyright.

The preparation of this book has involved obtaining permission for the reproduction of certain items. In nearly every case, a telephone call was sufficient and no charge was made. These permissions are acknowledged at the front of the book.

Libel

This is a false attack on someone's reputation. The courts can award very high damages for such defamation. Any book which contains personal criticism should be very carefully checked for the truth of its contents. A recent example is the case of *Slipper v BBC* (1990). In that case, Chief Superintendent Slipper claimed damages for libel on the basis that a TV film had portrayed him as a ridiculous buffoon.

BREAKEVEN PUBLISHING
June 199X

Dear Sir/Madam

I am writing to you to ask for your permission to reproduce a page from your book on bombing raids during World War II.

I am the author of a book entitled "Bright Memories" to be published by myself. The book deals with my own experiences during World War II.

I wish to reproduce a page of your book as a part of mine. I am not sure whether the copyright is owned by you as author, or by the publisher.

I would be most grateful for any assistance which you could give me in this matter.

Could you please let me know whether you would be prepared to grant this permission, and if so, the terms upon which it would be granted.

Yours sincerely

Harry Bright

Fig. 3. Asking for permission to reproduce copyright material.

Contempt of court

This covers threats to the administration of justice, including comments on trials in progress. In 1990, *Private Eye* magazine's publication of articles about a person who was suing it for libel was stated to be a contempt of court because it created 'a serious risk that the proceedings would be prejudiced'. The magazine and its editor were each fined £10,000.

Obscenity

This means material which 'tends to deprave or corrupt' and is a serious criminal offence. Only hard core pornography is now likely to attract the attentions of the police but publishers should be aware of, at least, the *Lady Chatterley's Lover* trial (Penguin Books), the *Oz Schoolkids Issue* case and the *Last Exit to Brooklyn* trial. These cases show that publishers of obscene material can run the risk of lengthy and expensive criminal proceedings even if eventually they are found not guilty.

Blasphemy
The offensive treatment of the Christian faith is a criminal offence. An attempt was made to prosecute Salman Rushdie's book *Satanic Verses* for blasphemy but the High Court ruled that Islam was not covered.

Privacy and confidentiality
There is no right to privacy in English law but publishers should be aware of the case of *Kaye v Robertson* (1990). The editor and publisher of *Sunday Sport* had organised the photographing of *Allo Allo* TV star Gordon Kaye in his hospital bed without his knowledge or consent. He could not stop them publishing the photographs but the Court of Appeal allowed an application under the ancient wrong of 'malicious false-hood'. This prevented the newspaper from publishing anything which stated that he had agreed to having the pictures taken.

The lengthy and complicated series of cases involving Peter Wright's *Spycatcher* book also centred on the idea of breach of confidentiality. The European Court eventually ruled that the protection of the efficiency and reputation of MI5 was not sufficient reason in the national interest to justify court orders against newspapers publishing information.

Racial hatred
The use of threatening, abusive or insulting words intended or likely to stir up racial hatred is a crime. Very few prosecutions have been brought. The consent of the Attorney-General is required but rarely granted.

Official secrets
This can mean the communication of almost any information acquired by civil servants under section 2 of the Official Secrets Act 1911. The National Council for Civil Liberties points out that it is a crime for an official in the Ministry of Defence to disclose the colour of the lavatory paper.

In November 1997 a former MI6 officer was convicted under section 1 of the Official Secrets Act after he offered a synopsis of his book to a publishing firm. The synopsis contained details of training operations, sources and methods.

Freedom of speech: the legal limitations

Does your book: *Possible legal difficulty*

(a) Contain other people's work?   Breach of copyright

(b) Criticise other people?   Libel

(c) Attack the courts?   Contempt

(d) Contain hard core
    pornography?   Obscenity

(e) Attack Christianity?   Blasphemy

(f) Give away secrets?   Breach of confidentiality
                                          and/or Official Secrets

(g) Attack ethnic minorities?   Racial hatred

CHECKLIST

1. Can you put your book through a word processor and produce suitable copy for a typesetter?

2. Can you transfer your manuscript on to a 'disk' that is suitable for typesetting?

3. Are you sure that your book does not break the law?

3
Preparing to Do Business

Publishing is not just a 'creative' process — it involves a range of practical tasks and paperwork which need to be dealt with in a very businesslike way. This chapter will therefore consider the following:

- keeping records
- naming your business
- producing business stationery
- deciding the title of the book
- sending out 'legal deposit' copies
- obtaining an International Standard Book Number
- keeping accounts
- getting further help.

WHAT SORT OF RECORDS SHOULD I KEEP?

'The strongest memory is weaker than the palest ink.'

From the start *keep every piece of paper* that comes in to your business and a *copy of every piece* that goes out. A desk diary is essential to keep records of daily correspondence and of future events.

Why good record-keeping is so important:

1. Misunderstandings and disputes can sometimes arise in business transactions. Clear and accurate records will help you resolve any disagreements, whether with suppliers, customers or anyone else.

2. It will save you time. An initial investment in time spent sorting and filing information in some kind of logical order will pay dividends as your publishing activity gathers momentum.

3. It will help you keep an eye on the main things you need to do, and avoid the risk of drowning in a sea of paperwork.

NAMING YOUR BUSINESS

Calling the business by your own name can be a selling point. You will be personally identifiable and this may generate interest in how you have gone about publishing your book.

Calling the business by a name ('imprint') other than your own may lead people to think your book was good enough to have had a commercial publisher issue it. The decision is yours and must be made early on for a variety of business reasons. The business name must be an original one and reference books in your local reference library of lists of publishers should be checked to ensure that the name you have chosen is not already in existence. Ask to see *Whitaker's Directory of Book Publishers* or *Cassells Directory of Publishing* (both annual publications). To have the same imprint as an existing publisher could cause immense confusion, particularly for bookshops ordering your book from computer read-outs.

Choosing a business name which has already been adopted by another publisher can also cause legal problems. In a recent case, a new publisher called itself 'Running Heads'. Many telephone and letter inquiries were sent in error to another well-established 'Running Heads' which refused to forward the inquiries and is considering legal action.

PREPARING BUSINESS STATIONERY

Letter heads
Letter heads could be printed showing your business name, address and telephone number. This can be a form of advertisement which will help to give your business a professional look. In *Yellow Pages* you will find a list of office stationery firms and it would be worthwhile shopping around to get the best deal. The amount of correspondence you will be involved in with the publishing of one book will not need a lot of writing paper.

Invoices
You will need some simple form of invoice to send with books you are supplying on credit (ie other than those prepaid). These invoices must be in duplicate so that you can keep a copy for reference purposes. The invoice should carry your business name, address and telephone number, although you could write by hand the relevant information as to copies ordered, price and so on.

Order some invoices early on so that they are ready for use before you offer the book for sale. This can then prevent delay when you receive your first orders.

BREAKEVEN PUBLISHING

Harry Bright

100 Success Street
Anytown AB1 2AB
United Kingdom

Telephone (01234) 12345
Fax (01234) 67890

VAT Registration No 000000000000

Fig. 4. A simple business letter head with the basic essentials.

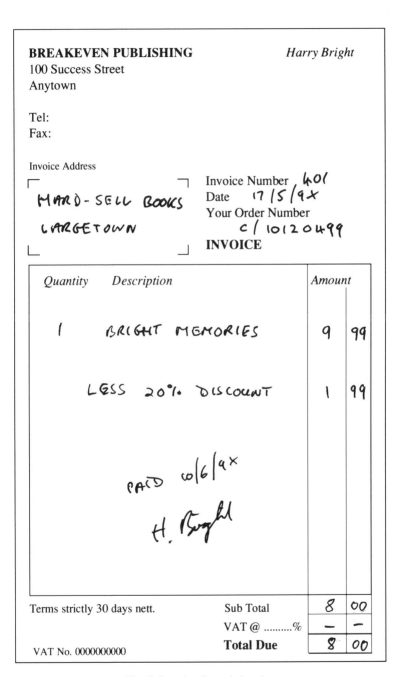

BREAKEVEN PUBLISHING   *Harry Bright*
100 Success Street
Anytown

Tel:
Fax:

Invoice Address

┌   ┐   Invoice Number 401
  HARD - SELL BOOKS   Date   17/5/9x
                           Your Order Number
  LARGETOWN   C/ 10120499
└   ┘   **INVOICE**

Quantity	Description	Amount	
1	BRIGHT MEMORIES	9	99
	LESS 20% DISCOUNT	1	99
	PAID 6/6/9x		
	H. Bright		

Terms strictly 30 days nett.	Sub Total	8	00
	VAT @ ....%	—	—
VAT No. 0000000000	**Total Due**	8	00

Fig. 5. Sample of a trade invoice.

31

Office stationery suppliers will have quite a selection of invoices for you to look over. Order the best style that you can afford if you want to project a professional image.

Padded envelopes

You will need a supply of these for direct mail orders and also orders from bookshops. You may need more than one size, depending on how many books are to go together. The envelope must be of good quality as it is annoying to the purchaser if a book arrives through the post damaged. This could result in a demand for a refund and affect further sales to the customer. A good quality envelope and books arriving in good condition will give your business a very professional look. You could get smart adhesive business address labels printed, to stick on the padded envelopes or Jiffy bags. See also Chapter Six on distribution.

DECIDING THE TITLE OF THE BOOK

You will have to decide the exact wording of the title early on if only for information for the various forms you will be filling in. A strong clear title can be a selling point and needs careful consideration particularly if the book has a local flavour. You can clarify the meaning of the title if needed by adding a subtitle, for example: 'Bright Memories: A Personal Account of Anytown in the War Years'.

LEGAL DEPOSIT OF NEW BOOKS

'Do I have obligations to send copies of the book to libraries?' — Yes, a copy of the book must, by law, be sent to the British Library at the following address:

Legal Deposit Office
The British Library
Boston Spa
Wetherby
West Yorkshire LS23 7BY
Tel: (01937) 546612

Send a copy off as soon as the books arrive from the printers to avoid forgetting your legal obligations.

Copies should also be sent to the following University libraries:

The Bodleian Library, Oxford
The University Library, Cambridge

The National Library of Scotland, Edinburgh
The Library of Trinity College, Dublin
The National Library of Wales

The above libraries are all entitled to a copy of your book and a request for them will come from an official agent. He is:

Mr A. T. Smail
Agent for the Copyright Libraries
100 Euston Street
London NW1 2HQ
Tel: (0171) 388 5061/380 0240/383 3540

OBTAINING AN INTERNATIONAL STANDARD BOOK NUMBER

You will find an example of this number on the back cover of this book, by the barcode. In this case it is 1 85703 262 4. Such a number (ISBN) can be allocated to your book and is used as a unique reference number, particularly by trade purchasers of your book. An ISBN is not compulsory but it is very much in your interest to obtain one. It enables booksellers, libraries and readers worldwide to identify your book and place an order for it. The first few digits identify the publisher, and the last few digits the title of the book. You will need this number for the printer before he starts work on your book. This means that early organisation is essential.

Notifying Whitakers

You can get the number allocated on a cost-recovery basis by writing to or telephoning:

Whitaker's Standard Book Numbering Agency Ltd
12 Dyott Street
London WC1A 1DE
Tel: (08911) 32100

It is essential to make a decision on the title of your book before setting about this operation, so that you can fill in the ISBN application form when it arrives.

BRITISH LIBRARY CATALOGUING IN PUBLICATION DATA

You will see this information on the front pages of many books (though not the one you are reading). It is a programme run by the British

From the Agent for the Libraries of the Universities of Oxford and Cambridge,
the National Library of Scotland, the Library of Trinity College, Dublin
and the National Library of Wales

A.T. SMAIL, Agent

Office Hours, 9.30 to 4.30
(Monday to Friday)

100 EUSTON STREET
LONDON NW1 2HQ
Tel. 071-388 5061 Fax: 071-383 3540
If telephoning, please ask for:
'Book enquiries'

How To Books Ltd
3 Newtec Place
Magdalen Road
Oxford
OX4 1RE

OUR REF: HPEWA/ww.

DATE: 30/9/9X

Dear Sir/Madam,   REQUEST FOR LEGAL DEPOSIT COPIES

On behalf of the Authorities having control of the above named Legal Deposit Libraries,
I request you to deliver to me, in compliance with the provisions of the Copyright Act,
1911 (1 & 2 Geo. V. Ch.46, Section 15), as set out on the back of this letter, copies as
shown below, please.

Number of copies required : 5

Title : How to Pass Exams without Anxiety Every
          Candidate's Guide to Success

Edition : 2nd   ISBN : 1-85703-055-9

Series :

Please send the copies of the above item, together with the attached copy of this
request, to me at the above address.

Yours faithfully,

A T Smail
Agent

Agency 23

Fig. 6. Request for legal deposit copies of a new book.

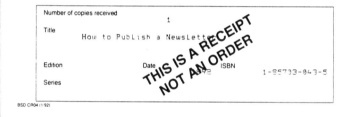
Fig. 7. Receipt for legal deposit copies of a new book.

35

Standard Book Numbering Agency Ltd.

12 Dyott Street · London WC1A 1DF · England · Telephone 071-836 8911 · Fax 071-836 4342

Harry Bright
Breakeven Publishing
100 Success Street
Anytown

15th June 199✗

Dear Mr Bright

Further to your recent application for an ISBN, the publisher prefix 0 9516344 has been assigned to Breakeven Publishing

The ISBN that you requested is as follows:

    Bright Memories Pbk.   ISBN 0 9516344 0 2

The ISBN must be printed with a space or hyphen between each part. It should be printed on the reverse of title page (under the copyright line), and on the back of the jacket, if one is provided. In the case of a paperback (with no jacket) the ISBN should be printed at the bottom of the outside back cover.

A Whitaker information form is enclosed so that details of this title may be submitted for inclusion in Whitaker's Books in print. There is no charge for this.

Yours sincerely,

for the Standard Book Numbering Agency Ltd.

Directors: D. Whitaker (Chairman), S. Whitaker, A. Mollison,
P. Allsop, L. Baum, R. F. Baum, R. C. Hunt
A subsidiary of J. Whitaker & Sons, Ltd. Registered in London No. 881964
Registered office: 12 Dyott Street, London WC1A 1DF.

isbn

*International Standard Numbering System
for Books, Software, Mixed Media etc.
in Publishing, Distribution and Library Practices*

Fig. 8. Allocation of an International Standard Book Number.

CIP Participants:
Please complete the shaded areas only and return with Prelims (title page, title page verso, contents page, etc). If prelim material is not available please complete ALL sections.

Non CIP Participants:
Please return the form fully completed.

Whitaker Book Information

Bibliographic Services,
J Whitaker & Sons Ltd,
12 Dyott Street, London WC1A 1DF

Contact name in case of query	
BRIGHT, HARRY	
Telephone number	

In most cases you will NOT need a CIP block. Simply put the following on the title page verso: British Library Cataloguing-in-Publication Data. A catalogue record for this book is available from the British Library.

Date of publication				
01 Day	10 Month	199X Year	

CIP Print Block required ☑

ISBN	Price £		net/non net	Cloth	Binding ☐	Other	Specify
ISBN 0951 634402	Price £ 9.99		net/non net	Paperback ☑		Other	Specify

Author(s) Surname first followed by other names	Editor(s) or Reviser(s) Surname first
BRIGHT, HARRY	

Translator(s) Surname first	Language from which translated

Title
BRIGHT MEMORIES

Sub-title

Height (in cms)	No. of pages	No. of volumes If sold as a set	No. and type of illustrations
21	180		

Edition (please tick appropriate box)	Name of illustrator(s)
☑ First ☐ Reprint	
☐ New ☐ Facsimile	No. of edition / Date of original edition
☐ Revised	Publisher of original edition

Name of Series		ISSN

Place of publication ANYTOWN	Whitaker special classification AUTO BIOGRAPHY
Whitaker general classification	Children's reading key

If the book is ADULT FICTION (please tick appropriate box)		Readership level (please tick appropriate box)	
☐ General	☐ Science Fiction	☐ Children	☐ Postgraduate
☐ Historical	☐ Short Stories	☐ Primary	☐ Professional
☐ Mystery (inc. Crime)	☐ War	☐ Secondary	☑ General
☐ Romance	☐ Western	☐ Tertiary	☐ Fiction

IMPRINT on title page BREAKEVEN PUBLISHING	Name and Address of distributor (if not the same as publisher)
Address of Publisher (if not a PA member) 100 SUCCESS STREET ANY TOWN	

In case of query contact Bibliographic Services on 071-836 8911

Fig. 9. Completing a Whitaker Book Information Form.

Whitaker/CIP
Book Information Forms
How to use them

Information supplied to Whitaker on these forms will be distributed by us to booksellers and librarians in 106 countries. Eligible book information will also be supplied to the British Library's Cataloguing-in-Publication programme.

The information will be published weekly, monthly and annually and will appear in a variety of Whitaker products including *The Bookseller, Bookbank CD Rom*, Whitaker's microfiche products and the bound annual volumes of *Whitaker's Books in Print*. The information will also be used by Teleordering to correctly route orders from booksellers and librarians

to publishers. Whitaker book information is also supplied to users by on line networks including Dialog, Blaise and BLCMP.

To ensure entry into the British Library's CIP programme, book details MUST be supplied at least THREE MONTHS in advance of publication. Provisional details concerning titles may be given, provided any changes are notified to us. Pre-printed postcards are available free on request for this purpose. Alternatively, please contact Bibliographic Services at Whitaker to discuss alternative proposals for updating.

Before completing the forms, please read the following notes:

1. **ISBN**
A separate ISBN is required for each edition. Full information concerning the rules for allocating ISBNs can be obtained from the U.K. Standard Book Numbering Agency Ltd, 12 Dyott Street, London WC1A 1DF.

2. **Price**
The retail price should be quoted in £ sterling. U.K. publishers and distributors should indicate whether the book is being sold as a net or non-net item.

3. **Bindings**
Apart from Cloth (or Cloth type) and Paperback, other major binding types are Leather, ½ Leather, ¼ Leather, Laminated Boards, Limp Cloth and Spiral. If unbound please indicate whether sold in folder, binder, box etc. If the item is a map please indicate whether it is sold folded or flat.

4. **Author(s) and Editor(s)**
The surname should be given first. Forenames or initials must always be given. If more than three authors or editors are responsible for the book only the first three names need be given. The names of "series" editors should not be given.

5. **Translator(s)**
The surname should be given first. If the name of the translator is not known the language from which the book was translated should still be provided. If the book is not wholly printed in the English language then details of the other languages printed should be noted.

6. **Title and Sub-title**
The full title and sub-title should always be given as presented on the title page. They should not be abbreviated or truncated in any way. If the book has a volume or part number or, in the case of an annual, a year of issue, then this should be given as part of the title.

7. **Size**
Please give the overall height of the book in centimetres. If landscape then the height and width should be given.

8. **Pagination**
The total number of pages in the book should be given. If prelims are present, and numbered separately, then the number for these pages should be given before that of the number for the main text, e.g. xv, 193.

9. **Illustrations**
Illustrations, diagrams, figures, tables, charts and maps should be noted. It should also be specified whether they are in black and white or colour.

10. **Edition**
A "First" edition is a text which is being published for the first time in a particular country.
A "Revised" edition is a text which is being republished with significant changes made to it.
Changes to binding, format, series or imprint may also have been made, but these, by themselves, do not entitle a book to be defined as a revised edition.
A "New" edition is the republication of a book where the text has not been altered to any significant degree, but where binding, format, series, imprint or title have changed.
A "Reprint" is the republication of a book where no significant changes have been made to the text and the binding; format, series and imprint also remain the same.
A "Facsimile" edition is an exact copy of a text, usually made by photographic or xerographic reproduction.

11. **Series**
Only names of series which are present on the title page should be supplied.

PTO

Fig. 10. Notes on Whitaker/CIP Book Information Forms.

12. **Imprint**

The imprint should be supplied, as present on the title page.

13. **Publisher**

The full name and address should be supplied unless a member of the Publishers Association, in which case only the name need be supplied.

14. **Distributor**

Details need only be supplied if they differ from the publisher's.

15. **Classifications**

A Whitaker classification should be provided for each book. If a title is eligible for inclusion in one of our specialist "in print" publications then the relevant special classification should also be provided.

If you are participating in the CIP Programme and you are supplying prelim material it is not necessary to add a Whitaker classification.

However the Children's Reading Key should be supplied for *all* relevant titles.

Copies of all classification schedules are available from the Bibliographic Services Department free on request.

Please ensure that the Bibliographic Services Department is on your mailing lists to receive copies of all promotional material and catalogues.

16. **Readership Levels**

Explanatory notes are available to those who require further information.

17. To obtain fuller details, or to order supplies of stationery, please contact:

Bibliographic Service Department,
J. Whitaker and Sons Ltd.,
12 Dyott Street, London WC1A 1DF.

Tel: 071-836 8911. Fax: 071-836 2909

J Whitaker & Sons Ltd
Bibliographic Services

Fig. 10. (continued).

WHITAKER BOOK INFORMATION/WHS SUBSCRIPTION FORMS

Information supplied to Whitakers will appear in the "Publications of the Week" listing in The Bookseller and in Books of the Month & Books to Come as well as the Classified Monthly Book List.

The information will also appear in Whitaker's Books in Print and in Bookbank, Whitaker's monthly CD-ROM Service. A copy of the Whitaker database is used by Teleordering in the processing of trade orders through their system. Other copies are used by organisations, in the UK and overseas, who make the information available to a variety of users via their on-line networks. Notable amongst these organisations are Dialog, Blaise and BLCMP.

Details should be supplied SIX to TWELVE weeks prior to publication. Provisional details concerning price and date of publication may be given. If changes are made to the details on the form, will you please ensure that we are notified at least two weeks prior to the last quoted date of publication. Pre-printed yellow postcards are available free on request for this purpose.

Before completing the forms, please read the following notes:

1. **ISBN**

    A separate ISBN is required for each edition. Full information concerning the rules for allocating ISBNs can be obtained from the U.K. Standard Book Numbering Agency Ltd., 12 Dyott Street, London WC1A 1DF.

2. **Price**

    The retail price should be quoted in £ sterling. U.K. publishers and distributors should indicate whether the book is being sold as a net or non-net item.

3. **Bindings**

    Apart from Cloth (or Cloth type) and Paperback, other major binding types are Leather, 1/2 Leather, 1/4 Leather, Laminated Boards, Limp Cloth and Spiral. If unbound please indicate whether sold in folder, binder, box etc. If the item is a map please indicate whether it is sold folded or flat.

4. **Author(s) and Editor(s)**

    The surname should be given first. Forenames or initials must always be given. If more than three authors or editors are responsible for the book only the first three names need be given. The names of "series" editors should not be given.

5. **Translator(s)**

    The surname should be given first. If the name of the translator is not known the language from which the book was translated should still be provided. If the book is not wholly printed in the English language then details of the other languages printed should be noted.

6. **Title and Sub-title**

    The full title and sub-title should always be given as presented on the title page. They should not be abbreviated or truncated in any way. If the book has a volume or part number or, in the case of an annual, a year of issue, then this should be given as part of the title.

7. **Size**

    Please give the overall height of the book in centimetres. If landscape then the height and width should be given.

8. **Pagination**

    The total number of pages in the book should be given. If prelims are present, and numbered separately, then the number for these pages should be given before that of the number for the main text, e.g. xv, 193.

9. **Illustrations**

    Illustrations, diagrams, figures, tables, charts and maps should be noted. It should also be specified whether they are in black and white or colour.

10. **Edition**

    A "First" edition is a text which is being published for the first time in a particular country.

    A "Revised" edition is a text which is being republished with significant changes made to it. Changes to binding, format, series or imprint may also have been made, but these, by themselves, do not entitle a book to be defined as a revised edition.

    A "New" edition is the republication of a book where the text has not been altered to any significant degree, but where binding, format, series, imprint or title have changed.

    A "Reprint" is the republication of a book where no significant changes have been made to the text and the binding; format, series and imprint also remain the same.

    A "Facsimile" edition is an exact copy of a text, usually made by photographic or xerographic reproduction.

P.T.O.

Fig. 11. Notes on Whitaker Book Information/WHS Subscription Forms.

11. **Series**

    Only names of series which are present on the title page should be supplied.

12. **Publisher**

    The full name and address should be supplied unless a member of the Publishers Association, in which case only the name need be supplied.

13. **Distributor**

    Details need only be supplied if they differ from the publisher's.

14. **Classifications**

    A Whitaker classification should be provided for each book. If a title is eligible for inclusion in one of our specialist "in print" publications then the relevant special classification should also be provided, as should the Reading Key for a children's book.

    Copies of all classification schedules are available from the Book List Department free on request.

    If your firm participates in the British Library's Cataloguing in Publication scheme then please supply the Dewey number allocated by them.

    Supporting descriptive material, brochures or dust-jackets should be attached whenever possible. Please ensure that the Book List Department is on your mailing lists to receive copies of all promotional material and catalogues.

15. **Readership Levels**

    Explanatory notes are available to those who require further information.

16. To obtain fuller details, or to order supplies of stationery, please contact:
    The Book Lists Department, J. Whitaker and Sons Ltd., 12 Dyott Street, London WC1A 1DF.

Fig. 11. (continued).

41

Library to list books before publication and make details available to customers. It is not compulsory. You need to allow at least three months before the publication date.

The CIP:

● creates a record about the book from information supplied by the publishers;

● lists this record on databases and in the weekly printed *British National Bibliography*;

● gets details of books to customers — public libraries, universities, colleges, government departments, companies.

BRITISH LIBRARY CATALOGUING IN PUBLICATION DATA

Pearce, David
  Blueprint for a green economy.
  1. Great Britain. Environment. Pollution. Control measures.
  Economic aspects.
  I. Title II. Marandya, Anil III. Barbier., Edward B.
  IV. London Environment Economics Centre V. Great Britain.
  Department of the Environment
  338.4'76285'0941

  ISBN 1-85383-066-6

BRITISH LIBRARY CATALOGUING IN PUBLICATION DATA
Research in education management and policy: retrospect and
  prospect.
  1. Schools. Management
  I. Saran, Rene II. Trafford, Vernon, 1938-
  371.2

  ISBN 1-85000-726-8
  ISBN 1-85000-727-6 pbk

Fig. 12. Two examples of CIP data blocks.

You should:

1. Supply accurate advance information about books.
2. Print an acknowledgement in the book, or the full CIP data block.

The acknowledgement should be worded as follows: 'A CIP catalogue record for this book is available from the British Library.' (See the front of the book you are reading for an example.)

KEEPING ACCOUNTS

Income tax
The best person to advise on income tax is an accountant. If the cost of consulting an accountant cannot be justified, then you will have to rely on your own research plus advice from the Inland Revenue.

The general rule is that all income must be declared, otherwise a criminal offence may be committed. In general tax is payable on any profits. Without going into the complexities of tax law, you should keep in an accessible form all documents concerning the financial affairs of the business. You should be entitled to deduction of any expenses incurred in the course of business, including stationery and printing, telephone calls, travel, postage, cost of running an office (a proportion of your normal household expenses) and professional advice. Entertainment expenses may not be allowable.

Value added tax
The dreaded VAT is a clever device whereby the government collects a tax without having to pay for the cost of collection. Collection costs are borne by the trader who registers for VAT. The tax is run by HM Customs and Excise. It must be treated very seriously. Remember that VAT inspectors have powers to search your office. The best advice is: avoid VAT if at all possible without breaking the rules. The typical small publisher will not have a turnover large enough (presently £49,000 pa) to attract VAT but the figures change frequently. VAT causes accounting and bookkeeping problems and a great deal of work. If in doubt seek advice from your local Customs and Excise office or from professional advisers. Assuming you do not register for VAT, you will have to pay VAT on typesetting and other costs if charged by VAT-registered suppliers.

Using an accountant
Running your own small business involves making decisions on financial

and tax matters. You may get general advice on this from your bank manager. The best person to help with detailed advice is an accountant but, as with legal advisers, good detailed opinions do not come cheap. Ask for an estimate of their charges or hourly rate before you begin.

GETTING FURTHER HELP

Local reference libraries usually have a large number of reference books such as A & C Black's *Writers' and Artists' Yearbook* which contains lots of information which will be of use to you from the business point of view. There are also books in the 'How To' series that can help you, for example:

How to Start a Business from Home, Graham Jones, 3rd edition 1994.
Managing Your Business Accounts, Peter Taylor, 4th edition 1998.

CHECKLIST

1. Have you made arrangements to keep proper records?

2. Have you decided on a name for your business?

3. Do you have a stock of business stationery?

4. Has the title of the book been decided?

5. Have you applied for an ISBN?

6. Are your tax affairs under control?

4
Designing and Producing Your Book

Many arrangements will have to be made to convert the edited script into a tangible 'product' ready for the marketplace. These can often take rather longer than originally anticipated, and you will need to plan ahead some months to be properly organised. This chapter considers the following:

- countdown to publication
- designing your book
- typesetting and proof reading
- indexing
- printing and binding
- using local suppliers
- deciding the selling price.

COUNTDOWN TO PUBLICATION

The best time to publish
The best time of year to publish is from the beginning of October until Christmas. This is the time of the year when the public buys most books, so that your book, to have the most sales success, should be ready for sale at least by the start of October. It might be just as well to get on with the process of making the book as soon as possible, even if it means that it will be ready well before October. After Christmas and the beginning of a year book sales drop considerably. Many bookshops are involved in annual stock-taking, and are more interested in returning unsold copies to publishers than in adding to their stocks.

Planning your schedule
Once you have decided the ideal time to publish, you should work back to devise a timetable to ensure you achieve this, allowing sufficient time for the various stages of writing, editing, design, typesetting, printing, binding and delivery. If it is very important for you to stick to a particular

date or month of publication, you are urged to plan your schedule well in advance, allowing plenty of time for sorting out problems along the way. So many things could knock your schedule off course, for example:

● delays in finding a typesetter able to use your word-processing disk
● alterations in design
● problems in deciding the cover design and completing the cover artwork
● holiday periods
● unexpected financial or legal problems
● loss of important material in transit (eg artwork or proofs).

Lining up your suppliers

These are the suppliers you will probably need:

Illustrator/photographer	_____
Designer for book and cover	_____
Proof reader	_____
Indexer	_____
Typing/WP bureau	_____
Typesetter	_____
Printer/binder	_____
Stationery supplier	_____

MAKING CONTRACTS

Many of the arrangements which you will have to make will involve legally-binding contracts. Agreements to pay cash in return for goods or services can be strictly enforced by the courts. Above all, remember:

● Contracts do not have to be in writing, so be careful what you say to customers or suppliers. The courts will give effect to a verbal agreement if there is enough proof of the parties' intentions.

● Never sign a written agreement unless you have read it carefully and really understand it all. It may contain small print which commits you to obligations which you never even thought about. Estimates from printers often contain 'standard conditions' on the back.

STAGES OF BOOK PRODUCTION

Script   *Complete by (date)*
Finish writing and editing   _____
Obtain illustrations   _____
Obtain permission to reproduce any
   copyright material   _____
Type or WP script in readiness for
   typesetter   _____

Design
Obtain competitive estimates from
   designers   _____
Design the cover   _____
Design the insides of the book
   ('specimen page')   _____

Typesetting
Obtain competitive estimates from
   typesetters   _____
Order typesetting   _____
Check proofs   _____
Prepare index entries   _____
Check index proof   _____
Ensure typesetting corrections all
   carried out   _____
'Camera ready copy' of insides then
   ready   _____

Printing and binding (book and cover)
Obtain competitive estimates for printing
   book and cover, and binding   _____
Decide quantity to be printed/bound   _____
Place order for printing/binding   _____
Delivery   _____

Accounts
Receive and pay suppliers' invoices   _____
Keep accounts records   _____
Keep all correspondence/estimates   _____

Fig. 13. The stages of book production.

● If in doubt, see a lawyer. But watch the cost of professional advice, which can often be in the range £80 to £150 per hour.

● Keep copies of all letters and other documents in case of disputes later on.

Royalty contracts

An agreement for royalties is the most usual form of arrangement between publishers and authors. Of course, if you are publishing your own book, you will not need to make a contract with yourself. But if your publishing venture involves someone else's creative efforts — text, artwork, design — you would be strongly advised to draw up a contract which covers most eventualities and which could avoid expensive and embarrassing problems if things don't go according to plan.

A copyright is itself a form of property — 'intellectual property' — and may be licensed (rather as if it were being rented out), bought and sold. An author may sell his copyright outright for example in return for cash payment. This sometimes happens in the case of very short publications (eg a pamphlet) or expensive illustrated books where obtaining high quality artwork may be more important to the publisher than the accompanying text.

Under normal author-publisher contracts, the author continues to own the copyright in the work (which was his by right as a result of the act of creating the work). The author then licenses the publisher to produce and market the work, paying royalties in return. In general, if the publisher ceases to do this for any reason, that licence normally expires, and the author would be free to license some other publisher to produce and sell the work. But the details of this are a matter of negotiation and agreement between the author and the publisher at the outset.

Unless it can be clearly proved that an author has sold his copyright outright (eg by a letter of agreement stating this), it should be assumed that the copyright continues to belong to the author.

A royalty is an agreed percentage of the retail or wholesale price of a book. The exact terms vary from publisher to publisher and from book to book: ten per cent is not unusual. Royalties on educational books or paperbacks may be less; royalties for best-selling authors can be considerably more. The contract may state that the royalty rate varies with the number of copies of the book sold. It should also contain the following clauses:

● length of the book (eg 25,000 words)

- date of delivery of the manuscript

- time for payment of royalty (eg 31 December each year)

- whether the author or the publisher is to have the copyright

- circumstances in which the arrangement will come to an end (eg when the book sells out, or after two years)

- what happens if the publisher goes out of business

- responsibility for the preparation and cost of indexes, illustrations, etc

- the handling of overseas and subsidiary rights including films and broadcasting

- publication of future editions.

DESIGNING YOUR BOOK

Before your book can be printed it must be designed. Decisions must be taken about page size, typography, layout, illustrations, type of paper, and similar matters. A printer may be able to give you some advice about this, but you could also use a professional designer. The designer can be the most useful person you come into contact with. An experienced one can advise you on the best proof readers, typesetters and printers. But first obtain a written estimate of how much he is going to charge you for his services, which will include:

- designing the inside of the book

- choosing a typeface for the book

- choosing the right paper

- obtaining or drawing any illustrations ('artwork') required

- monitoring the quality of work obtained from the printer

- designing the covers.

Book sizes

In theory books can be made to more or less any size, but the best value will be had from sticking to traditional book sizes such as demy octavo (about 215 x 135mm like this book) or A5 (210 x 148mm). Various smaller and larger sizes are available, designed to offer best value from the printing and binding equipment.

Binding styles

You will need to decide what style of binding would be most suitable, hardback ('casebound') or paperback ('limp').

Printing and binding are two separate processes.

Paperback
These may be:

- 'perfect bound' — not sewn, but glued using a thermoplastic process. Likely to fall apart with heavy use, but cheap. Used for most popular paperbacks.

- 'sewn limp' — which lasts much longer. Used for more expensive paperbacks.

- 'wire-stitched' — really just a couple of staples, only suitable for cheap booklets.

Hardbacks
Hardbacks, as you can well imagine, are much more (75-150%) expensive to produce than paperbacks. The decision is up to you but by all means ask for quotes from printers for both types. We cannot conceive of many situations in which an amateur publisher can justify the cost of a hardback edition. Public libraries often buy paperbacks nowadays.

Hardbacks may be:

- 'jacketed' — where the plain imitation cloth boards ('cases') are protected by a printed book jacket (sometimes known as a dust-wrapper).

- 'paper case' — where instead of having a separate jacket, printed paper covers are pasted directly onto the boards.

Hardbacks can result in more extra frills than paperbacks, for example:

(a) endpapers (including printed and/or coloured endpapers)

(b) decorative headbands (and tailbands) — coloured thread visible at the top (and bottom) of the book by the spine

(c) silver or gold blocking on the spine and front cover

(d) coloured top or side edges of the pages (eg in red or blue wash).

Most hardback publishers are busy cutting costs these days, and such extras are probably only of interest for special purposes such as limited editions, very high price books, centenary editions and the like.

Design of covers
A good designer will give much thought to this as it can be a very important selling point. If you look at the local books section in a bookshop you will spot immediately the books which have professionally designed covers.

These are some points to keep in mind when designing covers:

1. The actual words of the title *could* be a more important sales factor than the design itself — so keep a sense of perspective when wrestling with design decisions, and don't lose sight of your budget!

2. Colours. Printers may use one, two or four colour printing machines. If you want to use a colour photograph, this will mean four colours — actually four special colours from which full colour pictures are made up (magenta, cyan, process yellow and black). This is the most expensive option.

3. The spine is particularly important, because most books in bookshops are only visible by the spine. Make the lettering stand out clearly.

4. You may want to include a barcode on the back. It only costs a few pounds to arrange this, and may encourage bigger computerised bookshops to re-order.

5. Keep the design itself reasonably simple. Avoid over-decoration and embellishment. This should cost you less, and result in a more pleasing appearance.

6. The design concept should be shown first as a 'rough' or sketch of what is intended. When you have agreed this, it will be turned into finished artwork, ready for the printer to process. The artwork is usually presented on a sturdy sheet of card, with each colour often being shown on a separate overlay sheet ('separated artwork').

7. You could ask to see a colour proof of the cover, though this can be expensive and should be unnecessary if you have approved the design and the covers are printed satisfactorily. You may be offered a 'cromalin' proof or 'machine' proof. The former is really a form of photograph print, and the colours may not be a true match for what you require. The machine proofs are much better, since they are made using the actual colour plates, but because plates have been made the proofs are more expensive. Ask for quotes for the cost of these before you begin, if you think you might wish to see them.

Choosing a typeface

Good lettering can improve the readability of the book and thus have a beneficial effect on sales. A very wide choice of typefaces is available and selection is essentially a matter of taste for professionals. Popular typefaces for book setting include for example Times, Plantin and Baskerville. An enormous range of ornate or unusual typefaces is available for use as display headings, and a comprehensive set of these (hundreds) can be found in the *Letraset Catalogue* sold by major stationers or art materials shops.

Seeing a specimen page
If you are not sure about the typefaces being suggested, or which to choose, ask your designer, or the typesetter, to set up a 'specimen page'. This should show the following:

● size of page (dimensions/area)

● typeface to be used for text

● typeface to be used for headings (if different)

● arrangement of running heads and folios (page numbers)

● type justified or unjustified (normally justified in books)

● width of line of type (measure), eg 24 ems

- point size (depth) of type and leading (amount of space between lines). The text you are reading for example is set in 10 points within a line of 12 points deep, expressed as 10/12pts

- general appearance of margins top and bottom, left and right

- style to be used for chapter titles

- appearance of typeface variations (roman, italic and bold).

If in doubt, it is better to be conservative in your selections, and generally speaking the simpler you keep your design the better and more professional it will look.

Choosing the right paper

Good paper is an attraction. If you regard your book with pride do not purchase the cheapest paper on offer. The cheapest is 'bulky news' type which soon browns with age. Then come white offset papers (like the one this book is printed on), and finally expensive art (glossy) papers, mainly used for expensive illustrated books. If your book is to contain black and white photographs, you will need either a good white cartridge paper, or artpaper if funds run to it (perhaps an 8 page insert).

Computer-aided design and production

If you have a computer, or can borrow or hire one, you can avoid dealing with designers and printers altogether. You can type, design and print your publication on one machine. You can then do your own simple binding by folding A4 sheets into A5 and stapling them together. This is possibly the cheapest way of producing a book. In our experience it will, in most cases, come out looking like a student thesis.

Some publishers think that books will almost entirely be replaced by electronic information by the end of the century. One potential development is the CD Rom system which could hold an entire library on one compact disc. We do not share this view, for the following reasons:

- People prefer reading books to computer screens.

- Books do not depend on an electricity supply.

- Computers can go badly wrong — power cuts, faulty software, viruses.

- Computers can damage your health.

Plantin

Roman	ABCDEFGHIJKLMNOPQRSTUVWXYZ&ÆŒ ABCDEFGHIJKLMNOPQRSTUVWXYZ&ÆŒ abcdefghijklmnopqrstuvwxyzæœ .,;:!?"-()£$– 1234567890
Italic	*ABCDEFGHIJKLMNOPQRSTUVWXYZ&ÆŒ* *abcdefghijklmnopqrstuvwxyzæœ* *.,;:!?"-()£$– 1234567890*
Bold	**ABCDEFGHIJKLMNOPQRSTUVWXYZ&ÆŒ** **abcdefghijklmnopqrstuvwxyzæœ** **.,;:!?"-()£$– 1234567890**
Bold Italic	***ABCDEFGHIJKLMNOPQRSTUVWXYZ&ÆŒ*** ***abcdefghijklmnopqrstuvwxyzæœ*** ***.,;:!?"-()£$– 1234567890***

European accents additionally available

Characters per line

Fount size	Text Measure (width) in ems												
	18	19	20	21	22	23	24	25	26	27	28	29	30
8pt.	62	66	69	73	76	80	83	87	90	93	97	100	104
9pt.	56	59	63	66	69	72	75	78	81	84	88	91	94
10pt.	50	53	56	59	61	64	67	70	73	75	78	81	84
11pt.	45	48	50	53	55	58	60	63	65	68	70	73	75
12pt.	42	44	47	50	51	54	56	58	61	63	65	68	70

Fig. 14. Example of a type font.

Times Bold - abcdefghijklmnopqrstuvwxyz
ABCDEFGHIJKLMNOPQRSTUVWXYZ

Times Italic - *abcdefghijklmnopqrstuvwxyz*
ABCDEFGHIJKLMNOPQRSTUVWXYZ

Triumvirate Medium - abcdefghijklmnopqrstuvwxyz
ABCDEFGHIJKLMNOPQRSTUVWXYZ

Triumvirate Bold - **abcdefghijklmnopqrstuvwxyz**
ABCDEFGHIJKLMNOPQRSTUVWXYZ

Zapf Chancery - *abcdefghijklmnopqrstuvwxyz*
ABCDEFGHIJKLMNOPQRSTUVWXYZ

Plantin - abcdefghijklmnopqrstuvwxyz
ABCDEFGHIJKLMNOPQRSTUVWXYZ

Plantin Bold - **abcdefghijklmnopqrstuvwxyz**
ABCDEFGHIJKLMNOPQRSTUVWXYZ

Palacio - abcdefghijklmnopqrstuvwxyz
ABCDEFGHIJKLMNOPQRSTUVWXYZ

Palacio Italics - *abcdefghijklmnopqrstuvwxyz*
ABCDEFGHIJKLMNOPQRSTUVWXYZ

Rockwell Light - abcdefghijklmnopqrstuvwxyz
ABCDEFGHIJKLMNOPQRSTUVWXYZ

Souvenir Demi - **abcdefghijklmnopqrstuvwxyz**
ABCDEFGHIJKLMNOPQRSTUVWXYZ

Univers Extra Bold - **abcdefghijklmnopqrstuvwxyz**
ABCDEFGHIJKLMNOPQRSTUVWXYZ

Baskerville - abcdefghijklmnopqrstuvwxyz
ABCDEFGHIJKLMNOPQRSTUVWXYZ

Fig. 15. Extract from a typesetter's font list.

- 2000 compliance — left to their own devices, computers will crash at midnight on 31 December 1999. This is because they are unable to recognise the concept of the year 2000. Large publishers are at present investing massively in time and resources to deal with this problem. A complete solution has yet to be arrived at.

The human eye and brain can cope far more effectively with information in ink on paper than on a computer screen. It is statistically proven that proof reading from a paper printout is more accurate than that done on a computer screen.

We think that if a book is worth publishing, it should look like a book, as a work of craftmanship in its own right. We think that book design is not a job for the amateur. We would strongly advise engaging the services of a professional. With all the effort you are putting into your book don't spoil the ship for a ha'porth of tar.

You can keep design costs down by shopping around or by approaching your local Art College. Graphic design students may be keen to earn part-time cash helping you to design the cover, typeface, page size, paper and chapter headings. They may have creative ideas in relation to design which you have never even considered. If you think that this is being extravagant, look again at the local books section of your bookshop. The professionally-designed books stand out so well from the amateur jobs. They are proper books, not overgrown pamphlets.

A professional designer, if he is worth his salt, will be a meticulous artist who will insist on the most demanding and time-consuming attention to detail. Do not be exasperated by this — instead, build time for artistic thought and reflection into your schedule.

Finding a designer

It will pay to shop around until you find a reasonably priced designer but make sure that he is talented. Ask to see his portfolio. These are some questions you could ask the designer:

'How long have you been in business?'
'Which book publishers have you worked for?'
'Can you show me some book covers you have designed in the past?'
'Do you work with several different typesetters and printers?'
'What is the basis of your charging — by the hour/day? By the job?'
'I would like to see some sketches or roughs before deciding whether to proceed. How much would you charge for that? How much for the whole job if I proceed?'

BREAKEVEN PUBLISHING
June 199X

Head of Department
Graphic Design
Anytown College of Art

Dear Sir/ Madam

I am writing to you to ask if you could assist me with a design project.

I am the author and publisher of a book about my experiences during World War II. I understand that the production process of this book will involve a number of design matters. Would it be possible for you to advise me, in general terms, as to how I should go about this?

Alternatively, do you think that any of your students would be interested in becoming involved with the project?

I have a small amount of funding which I would use for design purposes.

I look forward to hearing from you.

Yours sincerely

Harry Bright

Fig. 16. Asking an art college for help with design.

'Do you draw diagrams, maps and other illustrations yourself? If not, could you get them done from my rough sketches?'

TYPESETTING

What the typesetter does

The main job of the typesetter is to prepare the text of the book in a finished form which can be handled by the printer. The vast majority of book printing today is by offset lithography, and the finished form required by

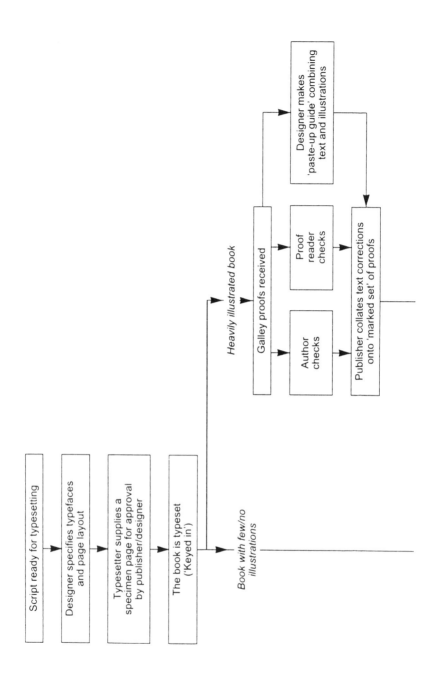

Fig. 17. The 'origination' stage of book production. Preparing text matter and illustrations into the 'camera ready copy' form required by the printer.

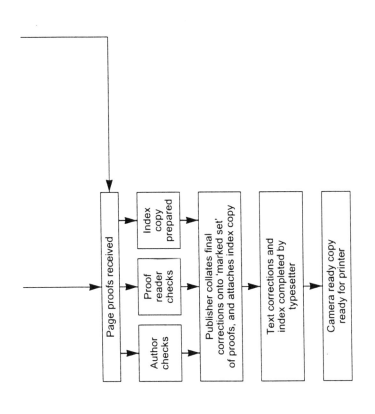

Page proofs received

Author checks

Proof reader checks

Index copy prepared

Publisher collates final corrections onto 'marked set' of proofs, and attaches index copy

Text corrections and index completed by typesetter

Camera ready copy ready for printer

Marginal mark	Meaning	Corresponding mark in text
⌐⌐	Transpose lines	⌐⌐
⌐	Cancel indent	⌐
⊏⊐	Centre	[enclosing matter to be centred]
↕	Set line justified to specified measure	⌐ and or ⌐
⌐	Move matter specified distance to the right	[enclosing matter to be moved to the right]
⌐	Move matter specified distance to the left	[enclosing matter to be moved to the left]
⌐	Raise matter	matter to be raised
⌐	Lower matter	matter to be lowered

Marginal mark	Meaning	Corresponding mark in text
⊘	Leave unchanged	- - - - - under characters to remain
New matter followed by	Insert in text the matter indicated in the margin	⋋
δ	Delete	/ through character(s) or ⌐ through word(s) to be deleted
(δ)	Delete and close up	⌐ through character or ⌐ through character e.g. character character
⊔⊔	Set in or change to italic	——— under character(s) to be set or changed
⊓	Change italic to upright type	Encircle character(s) to be changed
∿	Set in or change to bold type	∿∿∿ under character(s) to be set or changed
≡	Set in or change to capital letters	≡≡≡ under character(s) to be set or changed
≢	Change capital letters to lower case letters	Encircle character(s) to be changed

Fig. 18. Proof correction marks.

Table 1

Instruction	Marginal mark	Textual mark
Insert or reduce space between characters or words	⅄ ⊤	between characters affected / between words affected
Make space appear equal between characters or words	)—(	between characters or words affected
Close up to normal interline spacing	(each side of column linking lines	(each side of column linking lines
Insert space between lines or paragraphs	⅄ or ⊥ ⊤ or ⊥	
Reduce space between lines or paragraphs	⅄ or ⊥ ⊤ or ⊥	

Table 2

Instruction	Marginal mark	Textual mark
Substitute or insert character in interior position	/ or ⟍	
Close up	⊏⊐	through characters affected
Substitute or insert quotation marks	and or	/ or ⟍ — where required
Substitute or insert hyphen … or dash	Ⱶ	/ or ⟍ — through character / where required
Substitute or insert oblique	⊘	/ or ⟍ — through character / where required
Start new paragraph	⌐	
Run on (no new paragraph)	⌢	
Transpose characters or words	⌐⌐	between characters or words numbered when necessary

61

an offset printer is normally termed the 'camera ready copy', or 'CRC' for short. The text (incorporating any illustrations) is literally ready for the printer's camera — it is photographed, and from the photographic films are made the printing plates, and from these plates the sheets of the book are printed.

These days, typesetting is often done by specialist typesetting companies rather than by printers as was once the case. The printer will not be concerned with the contents of the book, or whether there are any mistakes in the camera ready copy — he will just go ahead and 'originate' the films and plates he requires. It is therefore very important to work closely with your typesetter, to ensure that the text and illustrations are all accurate and complete, and that the camera ready copy is all ready to go to press.

Choosing a typesetter

Yellow Pages has lists of typesetters. Shop around for the best prices. The designer you have hired could well advise you on a good one but check that he can handle ('interface') the disk of the manuscript if you have produced one. Many printers employ their own 'trade' typesetters or have close links with them. The cost of typesetting, that is getting the layout of the pages ready for the printer, depends on the quality of the copy and the type of book being published. Do not automatically choose the cheapest typesetter — you may find many more errors in the proofs. Some typesetters offer laser-printed proofs and laser-printed camera ready copy for the printer, to keep costs down, but the quality though reasonable is not as pin-sharp as that produced by normal computerised typesetting. Some typesetters charge by the hour, others by the page, or by the number of keystrokes. Agree the basis for charging corrections before you begin.

Using disks

You can supply the typesetter with a disk from a word processor, in which all the manuscript is electronically stored on a small cassette-like object. A manuscript then is set up for the minimum amount of work by the typesetter and because it avoids 're-keying' the job it can be the cheapest way to get it done. It is worth exploring because typesetting charges can be quite high.

Using a proof reader

It is worthwhile having your book proof read. No matter how many times you go through it yourself you will always miss mistakes, which could make your book look amateurish. It will not be too expensive (a reasonable rate per hour) and your mind will be more at ease knowing that your handiwork has been checked by a neutral observer. In fact, as you become more involved with publishing you will start to notice when you read other books, magazines and newspapers how many mistakes are regularly made.

An experienced designer should be able to advise you on obtaining a good proof reader. Designers will also be experienced in the use of computers for book design purposes and should be able to advise you on their application.

It is inevitable that you will have to do some proof reading yourself. Corrections to proofs should preferably be marked according to signs and symbols set out in a British Standard (see Figure 18). Copies of this Standard may be obtained from the British Standards Institution, 2 Park Street, London W1A 2BS. Many publishers mark typesetters' errors in red ink, and other errors or amendments in blue or black ink, to help check whether the typesetter's bill for corrections is reasonable.

How should I deal with illustrations?

Charts, maps, sketches and photographs can be worked into your book from the disk of the manuscript. Check with the designer, typesetter and printer on how they want this material presented to them.

Categories of illustration
- Line illustrations — drawings, maps, diagrams, cartoons and the like rendered in one colour (usually black).

- Halftones — photographs or coloured original artwork to be reproduced in black and white. An original photograph print is a 'full tone'; for the purpose of print reproduction it is 'screened', ie turned into myriad tiny dots visible with a magnifying glass, in which form it is known as a halftone, or sometimes as 'PMT' ('part mechanical tint'). Your designer and printer will agree which percentage screens to use. You may speak of photographs, but your printer is likely to refer to them as halftones or PMTs.

- One colour printing (ie black) is termed monochrome.

- Illustrations ready for reproduction are generally termed 'artwork'.

Tips on handling illustrations
1. Never mark original artwork, except well away in the margin, on the back, or on an overlay.

BREAKEVEN PUBLISHING
June 199X

Dear Sir/ Madam

I am writing to you to ask whether you could let me have estimates for the production of a book provisionally entitled 'Bright Memories'. The expected details are as follows:

Quantity required:	500 or 1000
Page extent:	184 pages approx.
Paper:	Good quality white paper
Page size:	About 25 x 15cms
Illustrations:	Yet to be decided
Binding:	Paperback
Covers:	To be printed in two colours and laminated
Delivery:	To my address as above

Could you please also let me know whether you could undertake typesetting, and if so what the estimated costs would be for the above work, including proofs.

The script and illustrations are available now, and we aim to publish the book before the end of September.

Yours faithfully

Harry Bright

Fig. 19. Approaching a printer for a production estimate.

FLASH PRINT LTD
SMALLTOWN

24 June 199X
Harry Bright
Breakeven Publishing   Estimate no: 123456

For the attention of Mr Bright

Bright Memories

Trimmed size   :   216 x 138 mm (Demy Octavo)
Extent :   184 pages

We thank you for your enquiry and have pleasure in submitting our estimate as detailed below:
   From line camera ready copy make negatives and plates, print
   by web offset in black ink, we supply paper quality book Wove
   80 gsm
   Unsewn. Limpbound – cover drawn on, glued at spine with hinge front
   and back

       500 limp copies . . . .£   800.00
       1000 limp copies . . . .£ 1000.00
       100 run-on limp . . . .£   70.00

   Covers
   Reproduction: from colour separated line artwork make final film.
   (Reproduction costs subject to sight of copy)......£81.00
   Printing: From final film print 2 colours one side only on our white one
   sided artboard 240gsm. Film laminate one side only.

   Up to 1000 copies – £   300.00   100 run-on – £   15.00

Delivery to Anytown inclusive.

Prices remain firm until 30 April 199X, but subject to price fluctuations of materials.

If we can help you further please do not hesitate to contact the undersigned who will be only too pleased to assist you.

Yours faithfully

Estimator

This estimate is given subject to the Terms and Conditions noted overleaf. Unless otherwise stated, all prices quoted are tax-exclusive and VAT must be added where applicable.

Fig. 20. Sample estimate from printer (first example).

65

Smart Print Limited
(Book Printers and Phototypesetters)
Largetown

Date: 18th June 199X   Our Ref.: CRM/JH   Your Ref.:

ESTIMATE No. 3/1046.
Subject to our conditions of contract printed overleaf

PUBLISHER   BREAKEVEN PUBLISHING

TITLE   BRIGHT MEMORIES

TPS: 216 x 138 176 pp (even working)	500 Copies	500 Run On
From manuscript set type in typeface and size to be agreed. Supply 4 sets of proofs.	£7.00 per page	
From complete CRC supplied, make negatives, plates and print in black line.	£450.00	£60.00
Supply 80gsm Bookwove. (Price ruling at date of estimate).	£150.00	£95.00
From flat artwork supplied print cover in 1-colour on 250 gsm board, jacket art and laminate (subject to sight of artwork).	£250.00	£55.00
Fold, gather and perfect bind. Draw on covers, trim pack and deliver Bristol.	£210.00	£65.00

For and on behalf of
SMART PRINT LIMITED

Company Registered in England:
VAT Registration No. 00000   Director: A. Smart

Fig. 21. Sample estimate from printer (second example).

Cheap Publications Limited

Directors: **Registered Office**
A. Cheap   Cheap Street
B. Cheap   Anytown

Registered No. **Telephone:** Anytown 332211

Harry Bright
Breakeven Publishing

12th June 199X

Dear Harry,

I have pleasure in enclosing the quotation for the printing of your publication. 184 pages plus cover, A5, camera-ready artwork supplied by yourselves, with us to neg, plate, print and bind.

Materials: text 80gsm tri-offset, cover 240gsm 2 colours, laminated, perfect bound.

500 copies £1,250.00 1000 copies £1,900.00

The above figures are provided half the amount is paid before production is started and the remainder to be paid within 60 days of receipt of invoice. The figures below are for payment of the full amount within 60 days with no amount paid before production is started.

500 copies £1,300.00 1000 copies £1,950.00

I hope that these prices are of interest to you.

Yours sincerely

F. Loggitt

Sales Representative

Fig. 22. Sample estimate from printer (third example).

2. You will save money if illustrations are a similar size, so they can be photographed by the printer all together (for 'common reduction') rather than separately.

3. They will be handled by the printer and may not be returned to you in pristine condition.

4. Ensure you have the permission of copyright owners to reproduce their work.

5. Where originals are to be reduced, the reduction is normally expressed as a percentage. For example a picture to be reproduced half size can be marked '50% reduction' and so on. Pictures to be reproduced same size can simply be marked 's/s'.

6. Forget using colour inside books — it is normally extremely expensive to originate and to print, and requires more expensive paper.

PRINTING AND BINDING THE BOOK

Choosing a printer/binder

Printing and binding is the most expensive part of the operation. You will need to shop around for the best price and also the best service. A good starting point is *Yellow Pages*, which carries a large number of local firms which can be contacted for the relevant information. The British Printing Industries Federation publishes a list of book and learned journal printers, specifying the facilities which they offer. This is available free.

Some firms can even offer quotes for turning handwritten manuscripts into book form but this could be extremely expensive and need strict cash and quality control. Your designer should be invaluable in your dealings with the printer because his reputation will be at stake, particularly in regard to the end quality, so that he should be able to give good advice on your selection. It is worth getting five or six quotes from printers. Some will offer package deals for the whole operation and you will find surprising differences in price — as much as 100% — and in the quality of advice and information offered to you.

TWO KEY PUBLISHING DECISIONS: PRICE AND PRINT RUN

Your discussions with the printer will involve answering two questions which go to the heart of publishing, and which even the most experienced publishers often find it most difficult to deal with.

1. How many books should I print?

The technical term for the quantity to be printed is the print run. You will soon discover that most printers will not accept orders for fewer than 500 copies of a normal book. A further complication is that the price for 1,000 copies will be less than twice that for 500, because there are initial setting up costs which are only incurred once. Because of the lower unit cost it is tempting to go for 1,000, but remember that you can always ask the printer to run off (reprint) more copies in the (probably unlikely) event that you sell out. Also, remember that experienced professional publishers can come badly unstuck in their decisions on the number of copies to be printed. Some printers will not produce less than 1,000 copies.

Here are some tips to help you decide how many to print:

- Unless you have a large number of definite advance orders, you will be publishing quite speculatively. What reason have you to think that 10,000, or 1,000, 100 — or even 50 — people will be prepared to purchase a copy of the book?

- The commonest mistake made by beginners to publishing is to print too many copies, often far too many. Remember, you can always reprint. Keep your initial order to the minimum. Don't pluck figures out of the air. Far better to sell out (problem of success) than to have half a ton of unsold copies in your garage (problem of failure).

- Rather than having a large print run, how about having a higher retail price, but fewer copies to sell? Price will only be one of several factors in people's minds when deciding whether or not to purchase.

- The people who stand to gain most from large print runs are printers, remainder merchants and paper-pulpers.

2. How do I decide the price?

You will have to decide the price at an early stage because it should really appear on the cover. Some books on do-it-yourself publishing contain detailed formulae for working out prices. We do not think that this is useful. Commercial publishers often speak of a 'mark up' of say six to seven times the unit production cost. One publisher says his policy is to think of the very highest price he could charge, take a deep breath, then double it.

When it comes to pricing, a book is a product like any other. The crucial question is, how much will the market bear?

In our experience, it is more helpful to work out a minimum price based on total costs divided by the number of copies to be printed. This will give you a rough idea of the cost to you per book.
Total costs will include:

- production costs including printer's, typesetter's and designer's bills

- administration costs including stationery, postage and time

- marketing costs including postage, travel and time.

The next step is to decide what the market will bear. You should look carefully at similar books displayed in bookshops to get a rough idea of what other publishers are charging. If you are confident of selling, say 200 copies, then a difference of £1 or £2 per copy will probably not make much difference. An obviously overpriced book will not sell well but an underpriced book will lose you money. Remember amateur publishers have an advantage over professionals in that their overheads are much lower. If they chose to, professional publishers could tell hair-raising stories about underpriced and overpriced books and excessive print runs leading to pulping or remaindering (selling off very cheaply for sale through discount outlets, or overseas). See the start of Chapter 1 for a cautionary tale.

Finding out more about book production

The British Printing Industries Federation organises workshops on book production and has published an *Introduction to Printing Technology*. This book gives detailed information on every aspect of the printing process, from initial typesetting to binding, finishing and distribution. Not many small publishers however will want to pay its price of £50.

SOME QUESTIONS AND ANSWERS

Should I use local suppliers?
Your book production could well be organised by local suppliers and this could be an advantage, if only because printers' jargon can be very confusing. A local designer can be a big help and you can hold meetings and discussions to iron out any difficulties that may arise. However, if you hire a local printer to do your work make sure that he is used to book printing and binding (eg not just leaflets and business stationery) and that his quality is good.

ESTIMATE OF PRODUCTION COSTS

Specification
Title of book   Price
Number of copies to be printed/bound
Number of pages
Page size
Type of binding
Type of paper
Illustrations
Type of cover
Other

Required	*Supplier*	*Estimated cost*
Cover design & artwork	_____	£
Page design	_____	£
Typesetting costs	_____	£
Typesetting corrections	_____	£
Cost of original illustrations	_____	£
Cost of proof reader	_____	£
Barcode	_____	£
Printing	_____	£
Paper	_____	£
Binding	_____	£
Delivery	_____	£
Other	_____	£
Total costs		£ _____
		£ _____

Free copies to be allowed for: 50
Unit cost of copies to be sold: £
Add unit cost of royalty: £ _____
Total unit cost of book: £ _____

Fig. 23. There are many ways of preparing production estimates.
This is one example of how to go about it.

How many pages will need to be printed?
Some printers have representatives who will call and see you and will explain about costs, quality and any other information that you need.

Generally books are printed in multiples ('signatures') of 16 or 32 pages. When calculating the total number of pages which will affect the cost of printing (the 'extent') do not forget to include the 'prelims' (preliminary pages). There may be some or all of the following, in the correct order:

Half title	The title of the book by itself on the first (right hand) page.
Advertisement	
Frontispiece	An illustration on a left hand page facing the title page.
Title page	A right hand page showing the title of the book, author and name of the publisher.
Copyright page	Name of the copyright owner (normally the author), details of the printer, and name and address of the publisher.
Dedication	
Foreword	Eg by a well known person, commending the book.
Preface	Brief introductory note by the author, often including personal thanks/acknowledgements.
Contents	
List of illustrations	
Introduction	

How should I pay the printer?
Don't be like those large organisations in this country, both public and private, which delay payment to their suppliers for months with the result that many small firms are driven into bankruptcy. Be businesslike and pay your bills promptly.

By offering to pay half the printer's bill before work starts and the balance on satisfactory completion of the order you may get a reduction in the original quoted price. Offering to pay by cash can sometimes also have a beneficial effect.

Should I check the printer's handiwork?
When the book is completed it will need checking for quality and accuracy. The designer will have a critical eye and will be most useful at this time.

Even if the books are delivered boxed or shrink-wrapped, each copy should be examined to ensure that it complies with your requirements. If the colour is wrong or the books are at all damaged, return them immediately. The printer has broken the contract and if you keep them you may lose your legal rights.

These are some things to look out for:

1. Is the quantity correct?
2. Are the paper and binding materials as agreed?
3. Is the text well printed (not smudged, or very pale in places)?
4. Are all the pages there, in the right order, and the right way up?
5. Colours as agreed?
6. Illustrations as agreed?
7. No greasy marks on binding or pages?

It is not uncommon to find individual faulty copies (eg a complete signature of 32 pages missing, or printed upside down, or appearing twice in the same copy). The printer should credit you for such individual faulty copies, and 25% of the retail price is a normal amount.

Why do I need a good index?
Any non-fiction book needs an alphabetical index. The aim of this is to enable readers to find their way around the text quickly and efficiently. Some authors attempt their own indexes and come unstuck because of technical problems. If the index is to be anything other than short and simple, say 100 entries or so, it may pay you to contact the Society of Indexers (see Useful Addresses). They can advise you on a suitable professional indexer who can quote a price for a job. Alternatively, if you have computer skills and hardware, indexing programmes are available.

Note: It is important to remember that if you engage the services of a professional indexer who is a member of the Society of Indexers, the Society will have applied an accreditation process. If your indexer is not a Society member, there is no guarantee whatever of her or his ability. Ask them why they are not members of the Society.

CHECKLIST

1.   Has a proper contract been drawn up?

2.   Have you found a good designer?

3.   Can you cope with computers?

4.   Has a proof reader been contacted?

5.   Is typesetting under control?

6.   Does your printer understand your requirements?

7.   How many copies are you going to print?

8.   Have you worked out your costs?

9.   Do you know a good indexer?

5
Promoting Your Book

There is a host of things you will be able to do to promote interest in the new book, and attract customers for it. In this chapter we will discuss the following:

- using the basic principles of marketing
- planning publicity
- devising and distributing circulars
- contacting potential individual buyers
- contacting organisations and associations
- contacting local libraries
- getting in touch with radio stations
- writing to the newspapers
- contacting television producers
- seeking the help of celebrities
- using trade reference books
- entering for awards and prizes
- using paid advertising
- distributing leaflets
- other sales operations
- holding a press launch.

EFFECTIVE MARKETING

There is nothing magic about marketing, that is taking your product to its potential market. You should apply the principles of controlled aggression and positive thinking. You can market your book by the systematic and careful application of proven techniques. In general, these boil down to good management. Effective marketing involves:

- The basic concept — having a soundly based product in the first place. Who is the book intended for? Does it meet a specific need? How does it compare with any competition?

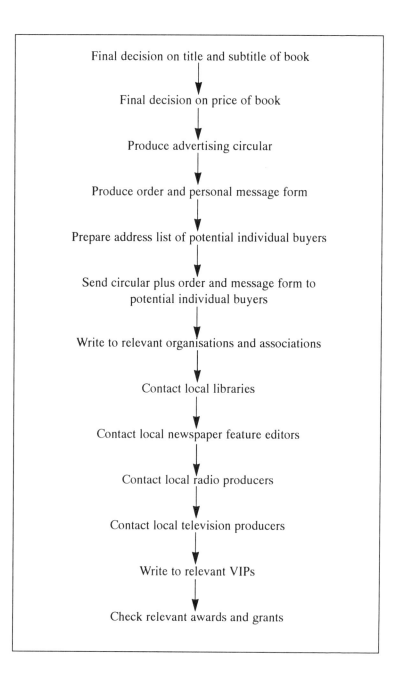

Fig. 24. An outline marketing plan.

- Planning. Your sales campaign should be planned in meticulous detail, otherwise precious time and resources will be wasted. Get your plan down in writing, with details of action, estimated costs and dates.

- Creativeness. Your advertising material should be lively, appealing, hardhitting, informative, and effective (see below, **using the AIDA principle**).

- Good timing. Make sure the book will be available several weeks before any obvious deadlines, eg a Christmas book by September or October.

- Thoroughness. Spend time compiling lists of possible outlets and customers, and keep the information in a systematic form.

- Making good use of all personal contacts.

The value of personal contacts

If anything could be sold effectively through mailshots and telephone calls and other general advertising, then large companies would not employ representatives. The reason why so much marketing is done by personal contact is that it has been conclusively proved that the most effective way of communicating is face-to-face. If you want to sell your book, you must get out and talk to people.

You could start with friends and relations, and move on to booksellers, librarians and representatives of associations. Particularly on a local level, you will find that most people are interested in talking to authors about their work. Remember that marketing must also involve an analysis of the competition. Well over 50,000 new books are published in Britain each year. They are fighting for the cash of the restricted book-buying public. How can you divert some of this cash your way?

Marketing, and to a lesser extent distribution (see Chapter 6), are the biggest problems facing self-publishers. But you can take heart from the fact that the professionals can get it wrong, far more often than they would care to admit.

Some years ago a professional publisher produced a technical journal based on market research which said that there was a definite need for such a new journal. Publication went ahead and sales were excellent. But the company's accountants decided that because the journal had not attracted enough advertising revenue in advance it had to close. Even their massive advertising budget failed.

PRODUCING A SALES LEAFLET/ORDER FORM

Using the AIDA principle
Sales professionals will be familiar with the long-established acronym, AIDA. It is very helpful to keep this in mind when planning promotional material:

- first attract ATTENTION   eg   'Local author publishes own book...'
- second stimulate INTEREST   eg   'Unique account of life in the Anytown Blitz...'
- third create DESIRE   eg   'Special pre-publication price...'
- fourth invite ACTION   eg   'Send off for your copy today...'

How to produce a sales leaflet
The easiest way to produce advertising circulars is probably from the printer of a word processor:

1. Using this method can make them seem more personal.

2. As they are so cheap to produce you can send as many as you want without worrying too much about the cost.

The circular needs to carry information very much like the back cover of the book, namely:

- the title

- author's name

- description of the book

- excerpt from the book

- the author's history

- the name of the book

- address and telephone number of the publisher.

It can also include any other information you would like, particularly of a local nature. The price of the book must be on the circular.

'I was fire-watching one night in the street outside our house when the Germans dropped landmines on parachutes. The first one exploded about half a mile away. When it did, a cylinder of flame shot into the sky above the houses with a terrific explosion. . .'

BRIGHT MEMORIES

Wartime memories of Anytown by

HARRY BRIGHT

Harry Bright's book is the story of his wartime experiences as a youth in Anytown.

His story starts with the outbreak of war. It continues with the bombing raids on the town and concludes with a graphic account of the victory celebrations.

The author was born in Anytown where he still lives and has many friends. He attended Anytown Reform School and spent most of his working life in and around Anytown.

BREAKEVEN PUBLISHERS
100 Success Street
Anytown
UK
Telephone
Fax

ISBN 000000000
Publication June 199X
Design by Anytown College of Art
Price £9.99 including p. & p.
Available from bookshops or direct from the publishers for immediate delivery.

Fig. 25. A simple but informative advertising circular. If printed rather than word-processed, it could include a photograph of the cover of the book.

'BRIGHT MEMORIES ORDER FORM'

I enclose a cheque for £......for......copy/copies of *Bright Memories*, price £9.99 paperback, including p & p. Every effort will be made to supply the book(s) as quickly as possible but please allow up to 14 days for delivery.

Signature: _____

Name (capitals): _____

Address: _____

Post code: _____

Tel: _____

PERSONAL MESSAGE OFFER

If you would like a personal message inserted by the author in his own handwriting on the front page of the book, please state your message below (not more than ten words):

Message:

Fig. 26. The basic ingredients of an order form. If used separately from the circular, make sure it also includes your address and tel/fax numbers. It is up to you to specify a maximum delivery time: if not supplied within this time, a customer would be entitled to a refund.

A separate sheet should be printed to state that if a book is ordered direct from you for cash it will have immediate delivery. The separate sheet will be the order form and a 'message' form with the offer of a signed copy by the author. This is something which large publishers can seldom offer but you as both publisher and author can, especially to potential individual buyers, and it is a strong selling point.

These information circulars and order and message forms should not be sent out until the book has been printed and bound copies are actually in your hands. Then, when orders are received — as they quickly will be when people know about the book — you will be able to despatch them immediately, particularly if the order is sent direct to you.

Immediate delivery is another advantage the small publisher has over the larger publisher because often when you order a book from a bookshop, particularly the large organisations, you are told it will take a month to be delivered, which can be off-putting.

Offering signed copies with a personal message

The order form with the offer of a message and author's signature, with examples of the message such as:

Best wishes John, or *Happy Christmas, Dad*

could encourage Christmas present sales, as a lot of books are bought as gifts.

These direct orders will probably be the most profitable, as some of the books can be delivered by hand and the others for the price of a padded envelope and stamp. You may even be able to accurately predict a minimum of advance sales, known in the trade as 'dues'.

IDENTIFYING INDIVIDUAL PROSPECTIVE BUYERS

Making your own mailing list

Having the book actually in your hand and having produced the information sheets, compile a list of individuals that you are going to contact. They are very likely to order a book from you, if only out of curiosity, because they will be most surprised to discover that you have published a book.

The list of potential individual buyers should include relatives, friends, colleagues, workmates, acquaintances and all the people that know you or know of you or have any connection with the subject matter of the book. A Christmas card list is a good starting point. If you want other addresses use telephone directories or other relevant records, if necessary spending some time in your local reference library.

The list of potential individual buyers can be extended to include schools (head teachers, subject teachers, libraries) and other institutions (director, secretary, treasurer etc).

Post one of the information circulars plus the order form to everyone on the list you have compiled and also get them handed around for circulation in areas where you are known.

Private buyers could well represent the largest outlet for sales of the book, so make sure that you maximise the list. Rack your brains so that no potential individual buyer is left out.

Commercial mailing lists

It is possible to rent mailing lists from commercial mailing houses, and if your publication has a high retail price and clearly identifiable market, this could be worth exploring. But the costs for one-off use are typically £100 to £200 per 1,000 names supplied on peel-off labels or other formats, and the response rates often only one to three or four per cent.

Free copies

Although it is not always easy to avoid, think very hard before you give copies away. Set yourself a ration at the outset (eg 10 per cent). People think more of books that they have bought than those they have been given. Be tough-minded. The time to give a lot of copies away may be in 12 months' time if they are just gathering dust in store.

CONTACTING ORGANISATIONS AND ASSOCIATIONS

Are there organisations or associations connected with the subject matter of the book, of which you are a member? If so, send them information circulars with a free copy of the book. Most organisations and associations issue newsletters throughout the year and they could review your book or write an article, which makes for free advertising. You could alternatively pay for an advertisement in the periodical, but first check the costs, the circulation sizes, and the copy deadlines.

Local reference libraries have a large number of reference books, such as the *Directory of British Associations* which you can search for leads. If you find any send them a circular and order form. Some associations and organisations have large numbers of local branches which could also be individually contacted with a circular and order form.

LOCAL PUBLIC LIBRARIES

Local and county libraries should be contacted. They are after all enormous buyers of books even in a recession. Send a free copy of your book plus an information circular and a covering letter to the head librarian of the specific library.

Public libraries usually have a section devoted to local authors, so a sale of copies is quite likely here. Libraries would expect some discount if they order directly from you but it is generally much less than you will have to give the bookshops. Usually they order from bookshops or library suppliers, but it's still a sale.

BREAKEVEN PUBLISHING
June 199X

Hon Secretary
Local History Association
Anytown

Dear Sir/Madam

I am writing to you to let you know that I have written and published a book entitled 'Bright Memories' which deals with my experiences during World War II.

If you feel that this book would be of interest to your members, could you please let me know?

In particular, would you be interested in reviewing the book in your members' newsletter?

Also, could you let me know if it would be possible for you to circularise your members in connection with my book, and if so, the terms on which you would be prepared to do so?

Yours faithfully

Harry Bright

Fig. 27. Approaching an organisation about the book.

Personal visits to public libraries can be both pleasant and profitable. Most librarians will be interested in your efforts.

You could also persuade your friends to enquire about your book at the desk of their local library. More often than not, copies will then be ordered and before long you will be gazing at your brainchild as it stands on the shelf in the appropriate Dewey category.

BREAKEVEN PUBLISHING
June 199X

The Head Librarian
Anytown Public Library

Dear Sir/Madam

I am writing to you to let you know that I have written a book about my experiences in Anytown during World War II, and that I have published the book myself.

I know, as a regular user of your library, that you have a section devoted to local authors.

I was born in Anytown, and my book contains masses of material with a local connection.

Please accept the enclosed copy of the book with my compliments. Further copies of the book may be obtained from me at the above address.

Yours sincerely

Harry Bright

Fig. 28. Approaching the public library.

USING THE MEDIA

Local newspapers

Reviews and features
If you can get your book anything more than a mention in a local newspaper it will have a major impact on sales. Most local newspapers review local interest books in a small way and this costs nothing but the best effect is achieved by contacting the feature writer of the paper responsible for local interest stories. Find his name from recent issues and telephone

him. The paper will have its telephone number somewhere, otherwise use the telephone directory or press directories in the local reference libraries. Then write to him enclosing a free copy of your book and an advertising circular. In your letter and telephone call, give information about your local life that might interest him to do an article about you and your self-publishing exercise.

BREAKEVEN PUBLISHING
June 199X

Features Editor
Anytown Evening News

Dear Sir/Madam

I enclose a copy of a book about my wartime experiences in Anytown, which I have published myself.

I would be most grateful if you could review it in the Anytown Evening News.

I was born in Anytown and have been a regular reader of your newspaper for the last forty years. I know that you print, from time to time, articles about local authors and publishers. May I telephone you to arrange a possible interview?

Yours sincerely

Harry Bright

Fig. 29. Approaching the features editor of a local newspaper.

If he becomes really interested he may want to interview you and have photographs taken. Should the local newspaper publish an article about you, make sure that it mentions the name of at least one local bookshop where your book can be obtained, or says that it is available directly from you. If by any chance you have any acquaintances in the newspaper world make use of them for advice on how to become known to the public.

An article in the local newspaper can have a major impact on sales. It is surprising how far afield local newspapers reach. For some valuable advice on attracting press coverage, see Peter Bartram's book *How to Write a Press Release* in the How To series.

Excerpts

Large excerpts of your book in local newspapers would earn you a payment at a standard rate as well as advertising the existence of the book.

Going further afield

Is it worth making contact with evening newspapers outside the local area? If your book has any reference to a particular part of the country or people there who might have an interest in what you have written, then it could be worth contacting the evening newspaper of a particular locality. The addresses of these can again be found in the reference books in your local reference library, such as *Willings Press Guide*. Send to *Letters to the Editor* a copy of your book, an advertising circular and a personal explanatory letter. It is surprising how many local people show an interest in a *Letters to the Editor* section of evening newspapers and if you can get your letter in print then it could result in sales.

Sending review copies to national newspapers

It is debatable whether it is worth sending review copies to national newspapers as they tend to review books only from major publishers. This is probably because those publishers spend money on advertising. If you wish to contact them, the addresses of national newspapers can be found in reference books such as *Willings Press Guide* in your local reference library. On balance, in our experience, we would suggest that the cost of sending free review copies, plus postage and packing, to the national press for review, is simply not worth it. On the other hand, you could strike lucky and receive a glowing review in a mass-circulation paper. This could mean that you sell out.

Approaching local radio stations

Local radio stations all have programmes in which well known presenters play records interspersed with interviews of people on subjects of local interest. Listen to your own local radio and choose a particular programme that would most likely be interested in you and your book. Find the producer's name from the programme titles at the start or end of the

ANYTOWN EVENING POST LTD
Grub Street, Anytown
Tel: Anytown 12345
VAT Reg. No. 0000000000

Harry Bright	**REMITTANCE ADVICE**	
Breakeven Publishing	*Account*	*Date*
	RU006CON	14 June 199X

INVOICE DATE	YOUR INV. NO./REFERENCE	OUR REFERENCE	AMOUNT
30/04/9X	BRIGHT MEMORIES	81124401	50.00
31/05/9X	BRIGHT MEMORIES	81624567	50.00

CHEQUE NO. . . . . 00034019 . . . . .   ENCLOSED   £ 100.00

Fig. 30. Receiving payment for the publication of excerpts.

87

BREAKEVEN PUBLISHING
June 199X

The Editor
Letters to the Editor
Smalltown Evening News

Dear Sir/Madam

I am the author and publisher of a book entitled 'Bright Memories'
which tells the tory of my wartime experiences in Anytown.

During the time covered by the book, I was in contact with a large
number of people who had come to Anytown from Smalltown. I
have lost contact with all of them, but I feel that the book could be
of very considerable interest to them.

If any of your readers remember their time in Anytown during the
war, I would be grateful if they could contact me at the above
address.

Yours sincerely

Harry Bright

Fig. 31. Approaching the editor of an evening newspaper.

programme or from the *Radio Times* or local newspapers. Write to the
producer and include a free copy of your book and an advertising circular. Follow up with a telephone call after a day or two or try to establish
personal contact.

If you have any contacts in radio circles make use of them for advice.
Success would mean you being invited along to be interviewed for the
programme. Being interviewed on local radio is an interesting experience and would definitely stimulate sales of your book. It is surprising
how wide a field local radio covers.

BREAKEVEN PUBLISHING
June 199X

Producer
Anytown Arts Programme
Anytown Radio/Television

Dear Sir/Madam

Please accept the enclosed copy of my book, Bright Memories, with my compliments. I am a regular listener to your programme and I know that from time to time you broadcast interviews with local authors.

I was born in Anytown and I feel that my book could be of considerable interest to your listeners. May I telephone you to arrange a possible interview?

Yours sincerely

Harry Bright

Fig. 32. Approaching a radio or television producer.

Here are some hints for radio interviewees:

- Ensure that you know where the interview is to be held, and arrive in good time.

- Be prepared: have a list of possible questions and answers.

- Keep it light! Relax and enjoy yourself.

Getting onto national radio

National radio tends only to deal with well known people. So unless you have contacts or your book deals with a very topical issue it is doubtful whether you will get anywhere with review copies.

Getting onto television

It is very difficult for an independent author/publisher to get any help from television. If you have any personal contacts they may be able to help you.

Local television services sometimes have presenters who interview local people with particular interests. If you have such a programme on your own local television station it could be worthwhile contacting the producer; his or her name would be on the subtitles at the beginning or end of the programme. Write to the producer enclosing a free copy of your book and the advertising circular. Your letter should include any points of local interest that might influence the possibility of your appearing on television. Follow this up with a telephone call later and you may even get through to the producer.

Appearing on television would be an exciting and rewarding experience and should help with your sales pitch.

APPROACHING CELEBRITIES

Send a free copy of your book, plus the advertising circular and a letter, to important people you know or know of you or could be interested in your book, explaining that you are an author/publisher. People such as your local councillor or your local Member of Parliament could help to spread the word around that you have succeeded in publishing your book and could well put your case to newspapers for some publicity.

Celebrities you might approach:

- local parish/district/town/county councillors
- Members of Parliament
- actors and other performing artists and entertainers
- leading authors in a similar field
- directors of major firms or organisations
- sports personalities
- television and radio presenters
- famous old boys/old girls of the local school.

Large publishers often approach well known people who have some connection with the subject-matter of a book, to ask them to write a Foreword. This is normally highly complimentary. There is no reason why the self-publisher should not use the same technique.

USING TRADE REFERENCE BOOKS

Your existence as a publisher means that you should appear in a wide range of directories and reference books which are essential tools for the

BREAKEVEN PUBLISHING
June 199X

Very Important Person
House of Commons
London

Dear VIP

Please accept the enclosed copy of my book, Bright Memories,
with my compliments.

I know that you were born in Anytown and that you have maintained
close links with the area. I hope that the book is of interest to you.

After numerous rejections by London publishers, I decided that the
only way to get into print was to do it myself.

Is there any chance of you arranging to review my book?

Yours sincerely

Harry Bright

Fig. 33. Approaching a celebrity.

printing, publishing and bookselling trades. Information supplied to
Whitakers will appear in the 'Publications of the Week' listing in *The
Bookseller* magazine, in *Books of the Month* and *Books to Come*, as well
as the *Classified Monthly Book List*. The information will also appear in
Whitaker's *Books in Print* (updated microfiche service) and in
Bookbank, an electronic information service.

APPLYING FOR AWARDS AND PRIZES

Use reference books at your local reference library to ferret out suitable
awards that your book might qualify for. If you should win an award

then this would increase your publicity as well as your income. A good starting point is the annual *Writer's Handbook* edited by Barry Turner and published in paperback by Macmillan/PEN.

PAYING FOR ADVERTISING SPACE

Advertising in the national or provincial press is costly and may not be worthwhile, but much lower cost advertising in the periodicals of relevant associations and organisations could pay off. Again check the cost and deadlines first.

When considering paid advertising space:

● Plan well in advance. Deadlines can arrive suddenly, leaving you too little time to make the most of the opportunity.

● For small display advertising, most journals will prepare the layout for you, based on the 'copy' (text) you supply. This is probably included in the cost of the ad.

● To assess the true cost of advertising, divide the cost of the ad by the circulation of the periodical concerned. The lowest price ad does not necessarily represent the best value. For example, an ad costing £100 reaching 10,000 people is probably better value (1p per person reached) than an ad costing £80 reaching 4,000 people (2p per person reached). But other factors may come into play, such as the quality of the readership, and whether the periodical is sold, or a 'free sheet'.

● With very limited space available, try to sell not just the book, but the benefit of owning the book, to the reader.

● Your ad will probably need a 'coupon' or little order form for readers to cut out, fill in, and send to you with their payment.

● Look closely at other advertisers' ads in the local press and see what you can learn from them, especially those that are repeated in many issues. Use one as a model for your own ad.

● Don't invest too much money in your first efforts — wait and see what results you achieve. An expensive advertising campaign can be a very quick way of losing money for the beginner, especially one offering just one low price product.

In general specialist journals, newsletters and bulletins probably offer the best value for the independent publisher with a specialist title to sell.

THE PRESS LAUNCH

Deciding whether or not to have a press launch needs careful thought. A press launch can easily degenerate into a party which will cost you money and sell very few books. Our general advice is, if you want to throw a party, wait until New Year's Eve; don't confuse it with trying to sell your book.

But it may be worth holding a formal launch if your book has a specialised market or celebrates an anniversary. Also, few people can resist the offer of a free drink. If you arrange a press launch you will need to consider the following:

- Will journalists be given a press release in advance?
- Do you have a list of press to be invited?
- Will you provide press labels?
- Can you get printed matter arranged in advance?
- Who will deal with tables, cloths, wine and glasses?
- Who will be responsible for setting up and clearing away?
- Will television or radio be there?
- Where exactly would the venue be?
- Avoid confusion as to the time and date.

CHECKLIST

1. Have you planned your marketing campaign?

2. Do your advertising circulars contain the right ordering information?

3. Do you have a complete list of potential individual customers?

4. Have you contacted interested organisations and associations?

5. Have you approached your local library?

6. Do you know who deals with features in your local newspaper?

7. Have you contacted local radio producers?

8. Are you in touch with your MP?

9. Which awards, grants or prizes could you apply for?

10. Are arrangements in hand for a press launch?

6
Handling Book Sales
and Distribution

Much of the work of publishing involves the practical business of getting the finished book into the hands of the eventual reader, through the wholesale and retail network, and through the library system. This chapter therefore looks at the following:

- dealing with booksellers
- doing your own direct mail bookselling
- selling to library suppliers
- selling to book clubs
- obtaining income from Public Lending Rights (PLR)
- warehousing and distribution of books.

DEALING WITH BOOKSELLERS

The vast majority of books in the UK are sold through retail booksellers, ranging from the big chains such as W.H.Smiths, Waterstones and Dillons to a host of smaller and specialist booksellers of all kinds. If you would like a share of this large market, you will need to be aware of several practical matters, for example on the terms of supply of books to retail booksellers.

What discounts should I offer?
All booksellers demand discounts varying, on average, from around 20% to 40%, depending on the type of book. Paperback bookshops may ask for lower discounts but the larger the bookshop organisation the higher the discount they require. Sales to UK bookshops are normally post/carriage free (unlike export sales). There are also special factors such as 'sale or return' which means that they won't pay for the books they've ordered until the books have been sold and you have to wait even after that for payment, perhaps until the end of a monthly accounting period. Any books that remain unsold after a short period will be 'returned' to

94

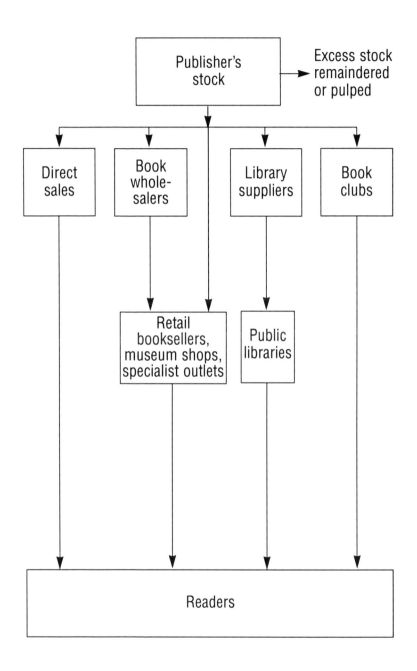

Fig. 34. The book distribution network. Getting the book to the reader.

you which usually means for a small publisher without expert distribution that you have to collect them. Apart from this inconvenience they
probably want a 35% discount. Bookshops will often send an order in
for only one or two books, obviously for a customer to the shop; you
may then get away with a lower discount. If you have dealings with a
particular shop you can check what sort of discount they expect from
you. Try some diplomatic haggling.

Approaching local bookshops
Individual local bookshops have to be visited and shown the book and
the advertising circular. They need to be informed of any advertising,
particularly if their name has been mentioned, perhaps in a feature
writer's article. Let them know that they can order by telephone from
you and have immediate delivery for any customer.

Local museum shops
These often have a section devoted to local books and could be buyers of
your title on a long term basis. It is worthwhile visiting a local museum
with a copy of your book and an advertising circular asking to see the
buyer and explaining what you have done. Explain about any advertising
and promise they can have immediate delivery by telephoning you.

Could your books be of special interest to different types of museums
with shops? If so, telephone the curator to ask if he would be interested
in your book; follow up by sending him a free copy plus an advertising
circular with a covering letter.

Check reference books in your local reference library for information
about museums and libraries. You can find out what type of museums
there are, whether there is a shop and the name of the curator. Tell the
curator that you will despatch orders very quickly. In return you should
find that museum shops will pay you very quickly and will expect only
a modest discount.

Bookshops outside the local area
The addresses of these can be obtained from telephone directories
(*Yellow Pages*) or from a directory published by the Booksellers
Association. It would be worthwhile letting these shops have an advertising circular and telling them that they can have first delivery by telephone ordering if necessary. You will find that there are a large number
of bookshops in your area.

As a result of your publicity you could have orders from bookshops
all over the country, with a great variety of paperwork.

BREAKEVEN PUBLISHING
June 199X

Curator
World War II Museum
Largetown

Dear Sir/Madam

I enclose a copy of a book entitled 'Bright Memories' which I have
written and published, in the hope that it will be of interest to you.

I know that there is a shop attached to the museum, and I wonder if
you would be interested in stocking copies of my book in the shop.
I feel that the book should be of interest to visitors to your museum.

If you feel able to proceed, perhaps you could let me know your
terms.

Yours sincerely

Harry Bright

Fig. 35. Approaching a museum curator.

Specialist booksellers

Your book could cover a specialist subject. To find out possible customers scour the reference books in your local reference library.

DIRECT MAIL BOOKSELLING

This is the most profitable method of selling. One advantage of publishing
your own book is that you can offer very quick delivery compared to larger
organisations whose delivery time is usually about four weeks. Hopefully
orders will arrive on the printed order form you have sent out, and all you

RETURNS NOTE

Always QUOTE **1**

Bookseller retains page 4 and sends pages 1, 2 and 3 to publisher for authorisation

TO _Breakeven Publishing_

FROM — _Megastock Library Suppliers_
Largetown Industrial Estate
Largetown

Listed by _____

Date permission requested _____

Date books returned _____

Method of return _____

PERMISSION GRANTED (WHERE APPLICABLE)
Signed for the Publisher

STANDARD ADDRESS No _____

PLEASE MAY WE RETURN THE BOOKS LISTED BELOW, FOR THE REASONS GIVEN:

QUANTITY	ISBN	AUTHOR	TITLE SERIES	INVOICE No	REASON CODE	RETAIL PRICE	INVOICE PRICE
19	0951634402	BRIGHT	BRIGHT MEMORIES		N	9.99	
			TOTAL BOOKS RETAIL				
			TOTAL BOOKS INVOICE				£189.81
			PLUS CARRIAGE CHARGE				
			NET TOTAL				

THIS IS NOT A BOOK ORDER

OVERSTOCKS

Permission from publisher needed for reason A, B and C and perhaps L

A Order duplicated by bookseller
B Recommended textbook that has been dropped
C Customer cancelled order
D Imperfect
E Received damaged

F Wrong title/edition supplied against invoice
G Wrong title/edition supplied against order
H From on sale/on approval/see sale
J Duplication by publisher

K As arranged with representative/by letter
L Old edition
M Recalled by publisher
N Other reason

Fig. 36. The standard form returns request note used by many booksellers.

98

W.J. SMART

From Don Page
Book Stock Manager
Extension 221

W.J. Smart
Largetown

Date: 25th August 199X

To: Sales Manager
Hopeless Books
Anytown

Dear Sir

We have recently reviewed all titles stocked at Largetown and I have agreed the titles on this returns request with ALAN STRICT, BOOK MERCHANDISE CONTROLLER and his buyers.

The titles listed below are surplus to our requirements and we wish to return this stock immediately.

951181602   Arthur Bloggs Railways Locomotives   £11.99
20 copies E

If you do not want the stock back, please let us know if you are prepared to issue a credit note to cover the cost of reducing the price of the stock for putting into a future sale.

Yours sincerely

Don Page

Fig. 37. Return of books: another example.

will need is a supply of good padded envelopes and postage stamps to send the orders off. The advantages of direct mail order are twofold:

1. No discount will be deducted.

2. You should receive cash with the order.

Copies returned by customers

Some books sold by direct mail order will almost certainly be damaged in the post. It is most discouraging when a carefully-packed batch of new books is sent back by the customer because the spines or corners have been damaged in transit. You may feel that the customer is being unnecessarily fussy if the damage is slight. You should note the following:

●   Replace any rejected copies cheerfully and without question or quibble as a matter of policy. Slightly damaged copies can always be used as review copies or for free publicity handouts.

●   Improve your packaging. Find out exactly what went wrong.

●   Consider alternatives to the Post Office. Commercial delivery firms will collect from your home or office, saving you queuing time in the Post Office. They will guarantee overnight delivery and their charges may be similar to those of the Royal Mail. The Royal Mail operates a Special Delivery service which costs approximately £3 per package. This service guarantees next day delivery. The package is computer-tracked, which means that if it goes astray, it can be easily traced by contacting a central telephone number. In the author's experience, this service is highly efficient.

SELLING TO LIBRARY SUPPLIERS

Libraries buy most of their books from library suppliers. These are large and active businesses which advertise their wares on a regular basis to libraries, and provide a range of technical back-up services. If your book is on loan in public libraries then you can receive payment from the Public Lending Right Scheme (see below). Payment is made by checking how often your book has been borrowed by public library readers.

So you can have two sources of sales income if a library supplier purchases from you. It will be very worthwhile for you to send a free

BREAKEVEN PUBLISHING
June 199X

Purchasing Manager
Anytown Library Suppliers

Dear Sir/Madam

I enclose a copy of my new book 'Bright Memories', of which I am also the publisher. A descriptive circular is also enclosed.

Could you let me know whether you would be prepared to handle this title, and if so, the terms upon which you would be prepared to do so?

Yours sincerely

Harry Bright

Fig. 38. Contacting a library supplier.

copy of your book, plus the advertising circular and a covering letter, to the head buyers at the library suppliers, with a request for guidance on how to work with them. It is worth following up your enquiries if the response from them is slow in coming.

These are some of the best known library suppliers:

James Askew and Son Limited
218-222 North Road
Preston PR1 1SY
Tel: (01772) 555947

B.H. Blackwell Ltd (Booksellers)
Hythe Bridge St
Oxford 0X1 2ET
Tel: (01865) 792792

T.C. Farries & Co Ltd
Irongray Road
Lochside
Dumfries
Scotland DG2 0LH
Tel: (01387) 720755

The Holt Jackson Book Company Limited
Library Booksellers
Preston Road
Lytham
Lancashire FY8 5AX
Tel: (01253) 737464

The Morley Book Company
Elmfield Road
Morley
Leeds LS27 0NN
Tel: (0113) 201 2900

SELLING TO BOOK CLUBS

These exist to supply their members with cut-price books, usually on the basis that a minimum number of titles is ordered within a set period such as 12 months. The clubs buy large numbers of books from publishers since they have relatively safe and predictable numbers of sales.

Sales to book clubs are normally made by publishers. If you can persuade a club to take your book (which to be realistic is extremely unlikely) then you can expect to sell out of your entire stock.

There is more chance of selling your book, if it is in a specialist field, to a club which deals with that field. There are a number of such clubs, covering subjects ranging from militaria to railways. See Useful Addresses.

INCOME FROM PUBLIC LENDING RIGHTS

If your book is purchased by libraries then a scheme called Public Lending Right (PLR) is currently in operation. Under this scheme, authors whose books are taken out by the public from public lending libraries are paid, by a sampling system, a small amount (currently 2.07 pence) for each time the book is borrowed. For the first year's payment your book must be registered before the month of June and payment if any is made the

Application for Registration

Public Lending Right Office
Bayheath House · Prince Regent Street
Stockton-on-Tees · Cleveland TS18 1DF
Telephone   0642 604699
Facsimile   0642 615641

NOTES

YOU MAY USE THIS FORM FOR SOLE AUTHOR BOOKS
AND TO APPLY FOR YOUR OWN SHARE IN JOINT
AUTHOR BOOKS - PROVIDING SHARES HAVE BEEN
AGREED.

IF YOU WOULD PREFER TO MAKE A JOINT APPLICATION
WITH THE OTHER CONTRIBUTORS YOU SHOULD COMPLETE
ONE OF THESE FORMS AND SUBMIT THEM
TOGETHER.

SECTION A
You must be resident in the U.K. or West Germany in order
to qualify for PLR registration - and this must be your
principal home. If you have lived in another country for any
part of the last two years, please give details on a separate
sheet.

SECTION C
You will have prior notification of PLR due. To save costs
payment will be made by credit transfer into a current bank
account. (We can issue a cheque upon special request.)

SECTION D
This section must be completed and signed.

SECTION E
This is required only on your first application for PLR and
should be completed by any professional person who is not
a relative and who has known you for at least two years.

* Full details on eligibility, co-authors, part shares, etc. are to be found
  in "Information for Authors" available free from the PLR Office, which
  should be read in conjunction with this form.

A Personal Details

| TITLE | Mr | Mrs |
| Delete or insert | Miss | etc |

Have you already applied for PLR? NO

PLR Author Number (if known)

Surname   BLOGG

Forenames   ARTHUR

Address   ANYTOWN   U.K.

Post Code

Daytime Tel. No.

B Author's Date of Birth

| DAY | MTH | YR |
| 4 | 2 | 46 |

Published Pseudonyms

C Payment Details: Bank Name and Address

| Account Number | Sorting Code | Account Name *(Current Account Only)* |

D Declaration I, ARTHUR BLOGG   declare the particulars contained in this form to
be true, and that I satisfy the residence requirements* of the PLR Scheme (1984 amendment).

My only/principal home is in,   UNITED KINGDOM   (country).

I confirm that the books listed under "Book Details" are published and eligible to be registered
for PLR* and I claim the right in them.

Where other contributors are credited on the title page, have you agreed percentage shares with
them?

Date   April 2, 199X   Signed

E Certificate

I, PAMELA MAY JONES
certify that the applicant has been known to
me for 10 years and that to the best of
my belief the facts stated on this form are
correct.

Signed   P. M. Jones

Date   2nd April 199X

Profession (with professional qualifications)

TEACHER - N.DD DA.mus

Name of Firm, Official Stamp
(if applicable) and/or Address

Fig. 39. Registering with the Public Lending Right Office.

103

Book Details Do not include any books until published.   Do not include previously registered books.

List on a separate line each writer, illustrator, translator, editor* and compiler* named on the title page, with the appropriate percentage share. Identify the nature of the contribution by use of one of the following as appropriate: illus; trans; ed; comp.

Co-authors who are dead or cannot be located must be listed here: please explain the situation and provide independent written evidence separately. *Editors and Compilers must have written at least 10% of the book's content or 10 pages of text and should enclose photocopies of title and contents pages (or other evidence) to substantiate their contribution.

Name of Author/s (as on title page)	Title of Book	% Share of PLR	Publisher	Pub'n Year (& Month)	Edn.	ISBN	For Official Use
ARTHUR BLOGGS	ARTHUR BLOGGS RAILWAY LOCOMOTIVES	100	BLOGGS BOOKS	JUNE 19XX	1	1- 85703-009-5	

N.B. You do not need to re-apply for editions (ISBNs) already on the Register.

Fig. 39. (continued).

104

following February. Further details of the scheme and an application form can be obtained from the Public Lending Right Office.

The maximum payment is £6,000.

To get your book registered apply to the Public Lending Right Office:

Bayheath House
Prince Regent Street
Stockton-on-Tees
Cleveland TS18 1DF
Tel: (01642) 604699

EMPLOYING SALES REPRESENTATIVES

Your book can be sold by employing representatives. They will contact booksellers and travel about the country supplying demand. As well as the discounts paid to the booksellers, representatives will expect a commission for each book sold, so that your income from sales will be drastically cut down compared with 'direct order' sales. Thus it may well be that you turn to representatives after Christmas when sales drop off. You will find freelance representatives advertising in publishing and book periodicals such as *The Bookseller*.

The Bookseller
J Whitaker & Sons Ltd
12 Dyott Street
London WC1A 1DF
Tel: (08911) 32100

Write the representatives a letter and ascertain what their services are and the fee or commission they charge.

WAREHOUSING AND DISTRIBUTION

Storing your stock

The storage of books needs careful attention. The printer will normally deliver in boxes of about 50. These should be kept in dry but not too warm conditions. The boxes should not, ideally, be stacked, because of the risk of crushing copies. Consider in advance whether you have suitable storage space and make appropriate arrangements. If you have a good relationship with your printer, he should be able to advise you on proper storage conditions. With a significant amount of money tied up in stock, you should consider insuring against the loss of stock, and the consequent loss of profit you would otherwise have made. Consult your local insurance broker.

Using a professional book distributor

If you are aiming to sell your book nationwide, or abroad, you may find it useful to do a deal with a combined marketing and distribution firm. They will take a substantial discount (for example 50%) for any books which they sell and distribute for you. If you add the bookseller's discount to this, let alone an author's royalty, then you could make a loss on each book you sell. In our view, this defeats the whole purpose of the publishing exercise. Many self publishers do not use distributors, for financial reasons.

'Distribution' — leaving aside 'marketing' — is normally taken to include:

- storing the stock in clean, dry, secure conditions

- picking out copies to fulfil orders

- packing (including the cost of packing materials)

- postage/carriage costs (Post Office, Securicor etc)

- issuing despatch notes or invoices with the orders

- dealing with returns for credit

- dealing with enquiries from the book trade.

CHECKLIST

1. Have you reached a decision on discounts?

2. Are visits to bookshops and museums being arranged?

3. Are you geared up for direct mail orders?

4. Have you thought about alternatives to the Post Office?

BIGG BOOKS WAREHOUSE
HUGETOWN

Arthur Bloggs
Smalltown

Dear Arthur

Here is a formal note confirming our distribution arrangements.

1.   BIGG BOOKS will act as the distributor for ARTHUR BLOGGS RAILWAY LOCOMOTIVES to UK bookshops.

2.   We will also endeavour to sell to shops outside the UK.

3.   We will take a discount of 50% from the retail price of £11.99.

4.   We will pay HOPELESS PUBLISHING 90 days after each monthly report of sales.

5.   We will give monthly sales reports, unless sales drop below 10 copies per month. In that case we will give sales reports every 90 days.

6.   We accept responsibility to collect all debts, equally we reserve the right not to supply customers who fail or refuse to pay us.

7.   The printer has informed us that they will deliver to us next week.

Yours sincerely

Brian Bigg

Fig. 40. Letter setting out distribution terms.

MEGA BUCKS BOOK COMPANY
NEW YORK U.S.A.

DISTRIBUTION AGREEMENT

Publisher: BREAKEVEN BOOKS   Representative: H. BRIGHT
Address: ANYTOWN   Phone:

Date: 2.20.9X

Inland Book Company, Inc., Distributor, will accept books on consignment from
_____BREAKEVEN BOOKS_____ , Publisher, on the following terms:

         X   55 % discount from retail price
(or)

            % of net received by distributor

Shipping from Publisher to Distributor is to be FOB Destination.

Books will be shipped to Distributor's warehouse at New York.

The sales period upon which reports and payments will be made is the first through the last calendar day of every month. Distributor will provide Publisher with a date Monthly Sales Report within two weeks of the end of every month, showing sales by and returns to Distributor, as well as books received from or returned to Publisher.

Distributor will pay Publisher for books sold 90 days from the date of each Monthly Sales Report. All collections on sales will be the responsibility of Distributor.

Distributor may at any time return to Publisher books received damaged or defective, postage or freight expense to be deducted from monies owed to Publisher. Distributor will pay postage or freight expense on all overstock returned to Publisher. Distributor will maintain, at its own expense, adequate insurance against damage, destruction or loss of goods while they are stored in its warehouse. Losses or damages incurred during shipment from Distributor to its customers will be the responsibility of Distributor.

Stock orders from Distributor may be in writing, or by telephone. Because Distributor advertises its services and stocklist to booksellers, Publisher will make every effort to fill Distributor orders promptly, and to notify Distributor as soon as possible when books are not available for shipment.

Fig. 41. Letter setting out distribution terms for the USA
(continued on next page).

Publisher will ship or deliver books to Distributor in uniform cartons whenever possible. Each shipment will be accompanied by a packing list indicating quantities shipped and book prices.

Publisher will promptly notify Distributor of price changes, publication date changes and all other pertinent information germane to its books and policies. When price changes are made by Publisher, Distributor will sell books at new prices, providing price stickers are sent when necessary; or with permission of Publisher, may sell current stock at old prices. Distributor may charge Publisher costs of labor when stickering is necessary.

Distributor may charge Publisher for services provided, such as stock transfers, books returned at Publisher's request, advertising, marketing and promotion, etc.

Publisher will provide Distributor with promotional materials as are mutually agreed upon, including advance or sample copies of books. Distributor will list all titles carried in its catalogs, and will advertise Publisher's books in its catalog and flyers according to Distributor's policies, based on discount received, as follows:

Publishers whose discount to Distributor is 55% of retail or 25% of net are provided a minimum of one and a half pages of advertising space annually; additional space may be purchased at its published rates. Publisher must provide camera ready artwork to Distributor's specifications.

This agreement may be cancelled by either party at any time after one year from its effective date, with notice in writing to be made at least sixty days in advance of termination.

A signed copy of this agreement must be on file with Distributor before books may be shipped. Distributor will accept for consideration all titles available from Publisher, but may choose titles it will carry at its sole discretion. Books shipped by Publisher without request or authorization of Distributor may be returned at Publisher's expense.

_____   _____

for MEGA BUCKS   for PUBLISHER

All checks will be issued to the name of the Publisher unless otherwise noted.

Additional terms:

Fig. 41. (continued).

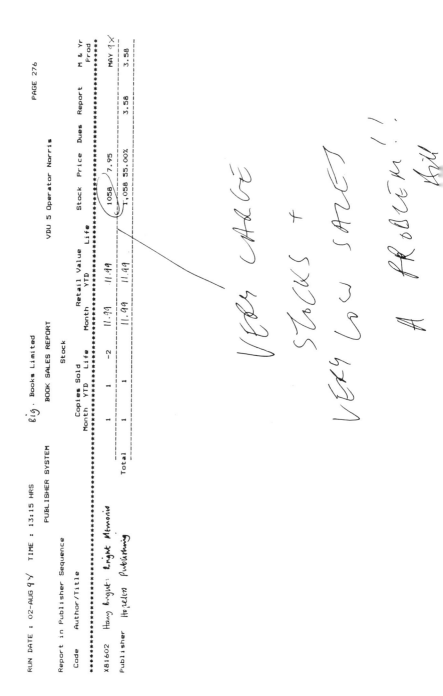

Fig. 42. A distributor's computerised stock report.

110

5. Have you been in touch with library suppliers?

6. Have letters been sent to book clubs?

7. Have you contacted the Public Lending Rights Office?

8. Have you thought about hiring sales representatives?

9. Are your storage and distribution arrangements in order?

7
Sales Records and
Follow Up

This chapter deals with the following:

● keeping a sales record

● filing

● making a financial assessment

● coping with bankruptcies

● collecting debts

● handling invoices.

KEEPING A SALES LEDGER

To run an efficient publishing operation it is essential to organise a simple record of orders and sales to customers. This will enable you to keep
track of whether customers have paid, or the date the invoice was sent
out; then at the end of a month, if payment has not been received, a
reminder invoice needs to be sent out. Checking payments from a list of
customers is very easy compared with rifling through dozens let alone
hundreds of loose copy invoices. Any queries about orders can be easily identified from your customer list. Have a customer list record book
ready for the moment that the first order appears.

Further sales and follow up orders can also be easily identified from
a customer list.

What form should sales records take?
Use a largish book with lined pages. Divide the pages up into alphabetical sections, about three pages to each letter of the alphabet for easy
access to information.

CUSTOMER LIST : BRIGHT MEMORIES

CUSTOMER	ORDER	AMOUNT	DESPATCH DATE	PAID
A N. OTHER PAPERBACK SHOP ANY TOWN TEL 00000 ORDER NO 111	1 COPY 31/10/9X	£8·00 (20% discount) INVOICE 25	1/11/9X	cheque 2/11/9X
MR A THE AVENUE ELSEWHERE TEL 00000 Telephone order	1 copy 4/11/9X	£9·99 INVOICE 26	4/11/9X	cheque 5/11/9X
A MAJOR BOOKSHOP OUT THERE TEL 00000 Order No 9999	20 6/11/9X	£124 (38% discount) INVOICE 27	7/11/9X	cheque 6/3/9Y

Fig. 43. Recording sales on a customer list.

113

Each alphabetical page should be marked off into five columns, to cater for the following headings:

Customer name	Number of	% discount	Despatch date	When
address	books	ordered		invoice
telephone no.	ordered	Actual amount		paid
Order No.	plus	charged		
	the date	Your invoice No.		

Every time you deal with an order, make sure you immediately enter the above details in your customer list book, otherwise you can become confused by all sorts of queries that are likely to arise. Always do this before you actually pack the book or books, because under pressure of work you can easily miss this essential part of the business.

Also ensure that when the invoice has been paid, the fact is recorded. Easy checking of payments can then be carried out and you will not have the misfortune of sending out reminder invoices to people who have already paid, which will not endear you to them. So don't ever forget to carry out this simple task.

FILING

As well as files for general purposes keep files of orders, invoices both paid and unpaid, and a separate file for the customer list book, which needs to be easily accessible as it will no doubt be the most used record.

File 1. Customers' orders will come to you on a great variety of pieces of paper. Keep them all filed away for reference if necessary. If you receive telephone orders make a proper copy of them and put them in the file. File customers' orders away when the actual order has been despatched.

File 2. Invoices awaiting issue, plus retained duplicates awaiting payment, should be kept in a separate file for ease of checking against the customer list book.

File 3. Invoices that have been paid should be kept in a separate file.

File 4. Put the customer list book in a well identifiable file.

Computer software is easily available to deal with accounts if they become complex.

COPING WITH BANKRUPTCIES

You can control your own financial affairs but you cannot hope to cope with the cash problems of your customers. Unfortunately as this book is published in 1998, small businesses are still going bust. The technicalities of insolvency law are outside the scope of this book but there are some points to look out for.

Limiting credit to customers
In general, do not supply large quantities of books on credit to companies which you know nothing about. If you supply, say, ten copies to a small distributor which goes out of business, you will probably be able to stand the loss. But if you have sent most of your stock to them, that will be the end of your publishing venture.

When a customer goes bust
In the unhappy event of a customer going bankrupt, technically not being able to pay its debts, you will receive a notice under the Insolvency Act 1986 informing you of a creditors meeting. You will be an unsecured creditor, that is, unprotected by a mortgage. Realistically, forget it. You might receive say 10% of your debt in a few years' time but it is not worth the time and effort of pursuing such a small amount. Put it down to experience and console yourself with the fact that bad debts may be deducted from profit for income tax purposes.

When the printer goes bust
The worst thing which can happen is that you pay half your printers' bill before receiving the finished book. At that stage the printer goes out of business. You will have lost your deposit and you will never receive the books. Again, this is probably the end of your publishing venture. In order to avoid this situation, be aware of the following:

● Try to ensure that the printer you use is well-established and efficiently-run. Ask to see other books which they have produced. You could also ask for bankers' references. Requests for bankers' references should specify an amount at least twice the proposed debt. Be on your guard if the bank reference does not include the words such as 'trustworthy', 'honest' or 'respectable'. Although bank references are not foolproof, they are free or cheap and are often the only way of checking up on the creditworthiness of businesses.

● Never forget that bankruptcy can strike without warning and try to build an element of this risk into your financial planning.

COLLECTING DEBTS

How do I collect debts from customers who fail to pay?

The bane of many small businesses is late or non-payment of debts. If a customer owes you money, you cannot afford to write it off. As a business person, you must act in a businesslike way otherwise you should not be a publisher.

The standard approach to debt collection is to send reminders monthly to debtors. But you may well reach a stage where such letters are a waste of time and paper.

Your next step could be to telephone. This may work in the case of small customers where the person responsible for payment is easily contactable. But with large customers this may not be possible.

Your last resort should be to the powerful weapons which the law provides for unpaid creditors.

Your final letter to bad debtors should contain a statement that if the debt is not paid within a certain period of time, then you will bring legal proceedings. It is important to stress to the debtor that you are not merely *threatening* legal action but that this will inevitably ensue if payment is not forthcoming.

It should state that this is not a threat of legal proceedings, but rather a statement of what will inevitably happen, with all concomitant consequences, if they do not meet their obligations and pay the invoiced amount in full.

If this does not do the trick then pay a visit to your local County Court. You will find the staff helpful. They will give you booklets to help you bring your own proceedings, for example in the Small Claims Court.

It is often said that the longer a debt remains unpaid, the less likely is it ever to be paid.

Points to remember

● If you have sufficient capital to start your own publishing venture, you will almost certainly not get legal aid.

● The cost of consulting a solicitor (typically at least £80 per hour) will almost never be justified in terms of the amount of the debt to be collected, certainly in the case of an amateur publisher.

BREAKEVEN PUBLISHING
June 199X

Managing Director
Pay Never Books Ltd
Largetown

Dear Sir/Madam

As you are no doubt aware, I have written to you three times with reference to the ten copies of 'Bright Memories' by Harry Bright which I supplied to you.

Despite these letters, and numerous telephone calls, you have failed to pay the amount stated in our invoice.

In the circumstances, unless I receive full payment from you within ten days, I shall have no alternative but to commence legal proceedings against you in the county court.

I should add that I am not concerned as to the matter of legal costs, since the proceedings will fall within the small claims procedure which I can easily deal with unaided.

Yours faithfully

Harry Bright

Fig. 44. Writing a debt collection letter.

● You do not need to see a lawyer in order to sue. The small claims procedure in the County Court is aimed at non-lawyers. It is relatively simple and can be used by any literate person.

● Even if you win your case, the debtor may still not pay. You then have a range of options through the court, including freezing the debtor's bank account or sending in the bailiffs to seize goods to the value of the debt. If the debtor is a company, you can petition to have the company wound up on the ground that it is unable to pay its debts.

● Do not be afraid of legal proceedings. The effect of a County Court writ through the letterbox can be magical.

CHECKLIST

1. Is your customer list properly prepared?
2. Have you prepared sales records forms?
3. Is your filing system under control?
4. Have you allowed for the risk of other people's bankruptcy?
5. Are your debt collection procedures in order?

POSTSCRIPT: AFTER EFFECTS

Because of his successful publishing venture, Harry Bright found himself something of a local celebrity. One result of this was that he received a number of letters from local authors, a local engineering firm and a community group asking him to publish their books. He sought advice from a friend who had worked in a commercial publishing firm. The advice was as follows:

'As a result of publishing your own book with the publicity it will receive, people may assume that you are a commercial publisher and as a result you may receive through the post offers of manuscripts of all types and descriptions, with a request for you to publish them. Do not be tempted because that way lies bankruptcy. Publishing is a risky business at the best of times, and the economic conditions are still difficult. To make a viable business out of publishing requires a deep pocket, a commercial ability to meet market needs, and much patience — to say nothing of long practical experience.'

Harry listened to this advice carefully, but was already beginning to wonder to himself whether to try publishing a follow-up title, learning from the valuable experience he had gained in publishing his first book.

In making a negative reply to an author be sympathetic in your refusal: remember in the past how you may have been disappointed when your book was rejected by the publishers. Recommend them to read *Writing for Publication* by Chriss McCallum (How To Books, 4th edition, 1997) and also this book.

It remains only to wish you every success with your own publishing venture, and to hope that you will achieve the particular objectives which have led you to explore the publishing option for yourself.

```
BREAKEVEN PUBLISHING
Anytown

Miss E. Evans
Llan Abertwm
Dim Parcio

Dear Miss Evans

I have now read the whole of the manuscript which you sent to me. I found
the material fascinating, and a very interesting record of your wartime
experiences. I think that there cannot be many such collections of material
in existence.

I feel sure that the Anytown Museum would be most interested in looking
at the collection, possibly with a view to publication. I suggest that you do
not let the original manuscript out of your possession unless you are
absolutely certain that it will be well looked after.

You might also consider approaching your Old Comrades' Association, if
one exists.

I note that you do not seem to have a telephone. This may be a disadvantage
in dealing with publishers and other organisations.

In terms of possible London publishers, I would suggest that you get hold
of a copy of the Writers' and Artists' Yearbook, published annually by A
& C Black. This book is extremely useful for authors wishing to get their
work published.

I do not feel able to take on the publication of the material myself, because
of the costs involved. You may remember that I gave you detailed infor-
mation about the costings for 'Bright Memories'. We have just about
covered our costs by having an intensive marketing campaign before
Christmas. I do not feel that we could do the same for your book.

In this connection, I should strongly advise you to have nothing to do with
any publisher who asks for money to meet the costs of his operation.

If I can advise you further, please let me know.

Yours sincerely


Harry Bright
```

Fig. 45. Replying to an unsolicited offer of a manuscript. Authors should be
wary of so-called 'vanity publishing' which should be avoided.

119

Glossary

A5. A standard size of paper measuring 210 x 149mm, equal to half A4 size (297 x 210mm).

Artwork. Any illustrative or textmatter in finished form ready to be reproduced by a printer. Often called **camera ready copy** or CRC for short.

Awards. Publishers and authors may be eligible for a number of cash awards, grants or prizes. See Further Reading.

Binding. Different methods of producing book covers to protect the pages inside.

Blurb. The publisher's description of the contents of a book and its author which appears on its cover and on publicity material.

BPIF. British Printing Industries Federation, printers' trade organisation.

Breach. The infringement of a legal right or duty.

Camera ready copy (CRC). Material set out on a page after all alterations, ready to be photographed for printing plates to be made.

Case binding. A hard cover binding.

Cataloguing in Publication. A programme run by the British Library to list books before publication and to make details available to potential customers.

Circular. Written information about a book, circulated to potential buyers.

Contract. The law of contract is the body of rules governing agreements intended to create legal relations, whether in writing or not.

Copy. Text matter.

Copyright. An author's, illustrator's or publisher's exclusive right to publish original written material or illustrations.

Copyright page. The page of a book which states the person who owns the copyright in the book. It usually also contains the full name and address of the publishers.

Demy octavo. A popular standard size for book printing — the same size as the book you are reading.

Disc, disk. A cassette-like object used to store electronic information for computers.

Discount. The percentage of a book's retail price demanded by distributors or booksellers in return for their stocking and selling a book.

Distribution. The physical business of packing and despatching books to customers. A commercial distribution service may also offer invoicing, cash collection and marketing services.

Dues. Publishers' term for orders subscribed in advance of publication.

Edition. The quantity printed of a book. An edition may be reprinted. A second or subsequent edition however will contain substantial alterations.

Em. A unit of measurement in typesetting and printing. One em is a sixth of an inch. Ems are used for example to specify the measure (width) of a line of type, eg 24 ems.

Excerpts. Extracts from a book which are published separately, for example in newspapers.

Facsimile edition. An exact copy of a book.

Feature writer. A journalist whose work is writing articles other than hard news.

First edition. See **Edition**, above.

Floppy disk. See **Disc**, above.

Folio. A sheet of printed paper comprising two pages or sides.

Font. See **Typeface**, below.

Foreword. A piece of copy in which the author of a book (or a third party) makes introductory or preliminary comments.

Frontispiece. The first illustration of a book, on the left facing the title-page.

Galley proofs. A first impression of a book, produced by the typesetter, which is not divided into numbered pages.

Gsm (grams per square metre). Standard description of paper by its weight. Book papers are typically in the range of 70gsm to 100gsm.

Half title. The first page of a book which according to tradition contains only its title.

Halftone. A photograph or other illustration consisting of a myriad of tiny dots visible under a magnifying glass, in a form ready for reproduction by the printer. For colour halftones, the dots are in the four **process colours**.

House style. Every publisher must make decisions as to the presentation and style of books. This is known as 'house style'.

Imposition. An arrangement of pages of type by the printer.

Imprint. Information about the publisher or printer of a book, inserted at the beginning or at the end of a book.

Indents. The setting back of a line of text from the margin of a page.

Index. An alphabetical list of the contents of a book, usually positioned at the end.

International Standard Book Number (ISBN). A ten-digit number, usually printed along with the publishing information on the back cover of the book, and on the verso (back) of the title page. It identifies the book for distribution and marketing purposes.

Internet. A worldwide network of computers.

Italic. Oblique type.

Justification. The adjustment of type to be parallel with the edges of a page.

Laminated. A laminated book cover is one which is overlaid with a protective film. Varnishing is a cheaper and lower quality alternative.

Legal deposit. A copy of every book must, by law, be sent to the British Library. See Useful Addresses.

Liability. Legal obligation or duty.

Limp. A soft cover of a book, now known generally as paperback.

Limp cloth. A more sturdy type of paperback with cloth reinforcement.

Lower case. Small, as opposed to capital, letters.

Mailshots. Advertisements for books which are posted to a range of potential buyers or reviewers.

Manuscript. Literally, a handwritten document. Now generally means a book as it is presented to the publisher by the author, whether handwritten, typed or word-processed. MS for short.

Mark up. Retail price divided by unit cost.

Net Book Agreement. An agreement between most booksellers and publishers that books should not be sold to the public at less than a minimum retail price. The advantage of the NBA is said to be that booksellers can keep large stocks of books in the knowledge that their prices will not be undercut.

Official secrets. Information restricted by the Official Secrets Acts. Covers almost any information communicated to a civil servant.

Offset litho machine. A printing machine in which the image to be printed is offset (passed) to a cylinder for the actual printing process. This is by far the commonest method of book production today, having replaced the old letterpress methods long ago.

Page proofs. Trial impressions of a book with numbered pages.

Pagination. The method by which the pages of a book are numbered.

Perfect bound. A method of bookbinding using glue, instead of sewing with thread.

PMT (part mechanical tint). Another term for a **halftone**, especially a black and white photograph.

Point. A unit of measurement in typesetting. One point is 1/72nd of an inch. There are 12 points in one **em**, and six ems to the inch. Type sizes are expressed in numbers of points, eg 10pt.

Preface. See **Foreword**, above.

Prelims. The preliminary pages of a book which come before the introduction or beginning of chapter one. Often these pages are not numbered as such.

Press release. Information about a book, aimed at and sent to newspapers and magazines.

Process colours. The four standard colours used for full-colour printing of artwork or photographs. They are black, magenta, cyan and process yellow.

Print run. The number of copies of a book which are printed at one time.

Proof reader. Someone who checks proofs for errors and stylistic discrepancies.

Proofs. Trial impressions of printed pages of a book. They can be **galley proofs** and/or **page proofs**.

Public Lending Rights. A scheme whereby authors whose books are borrowed by the public from libraries are paid a small sum for each occasion they are borrowed.

Rejection slips. Standard forms used by commercial publishers to inform prospective authors that their work is unacceptable.

Remaindering. The sale very cheaply of a batch of unsold books to a firm which specialises in cut-price books. Some book remainder dealers even have their own retail bookshops.

Repetitive strain injury. An illness caused by repetitive movements at work, especially typing and word-processing.

Returns. Books which have been unsold and are sent back by the bookseller to the publisher for credit. This can sometimes happen many months after they were first purchased.

Royalty. A payment made by a publisher to an author which amounts to a percentage of the price of a book, or of the revenue received.

Revised edition. See **Edition**, above.

Running head. A page heading which runs for a number of pages. See the top of this page for an example.

Sale or return. An arrangement with a distributor or bookseller whereby books are stocked on the basis that only those sold will be paid for.

Self publishing. Publishing work you have produced yourself.

Shrink wrapped. A method of wrapping books in plastic.

Tenosynovitis. See **Repetitive strain injury**, above.

Text measure. The width of a full line of type, specified in numbers of ems, for example '14 ems justified' or '18 ems unjustified right'.

Title page. The main opening page of a book normally showing the series title (if any), the title in bold letters, the name of the author and the name of the publisher at the foot.

Trade terms. Terms on which a publisher offers to do business with a bookseller including in particular the amount of discount, credit period and postage charges if any.

Typeface. A style of print. Perhaps the best known is Times, but most printers have a wide choice available. Well-known and widely used book typesetting faces include Times, Plantin, Baskerville and Bembo.

Typescript. Typed or word-processed material.

Typesetting. The composition of a manuscript into pages suitable for printing.

Vanity publishing. An arrangement whereby an author pays for the publication of his book.

Web offset. See **Offset litho machine**, above.

Word processor. A type of computer programmed to use its keyboard as a typewriter, to display words written on a screen, to edit and amend the words and to print them out.

Further Reading

An Author's Guide to Publishing, Michael Legat (Robert Hale, 1982).

Are Books Different? Marketing in the Book Trade, Alison Baverstock (Kogan Page, 1993).

Benn's Media Directory.

Blackwell Guide for Authors, (Blackwell, revised edition 1991).

Blueprint Dictionary of Printing and Publishing, John Peacock and Michael Barnard (Blueprint, 1990).

The Bookseller (Whitaker). Weekly trade magazine.

British Books in Print: The Reference Catalogue of Current Literature (Whitaker).

The Business of Book Publishing, C. Bingley (Pergamon Press).

Copinger and Skone James on Copyright (Sweet & Maxwell).

Copy-Editing, Judith Butcher (Cambridge University Press, 1993). A standard reference book.

Directory of British Associations (CBD Research).

Directory of Grant Making Trusts.

Directory of Members (Booksellers Association, annual).

Directory of Publishing (Cassell, annual).

Editing, Design and Book Production, Charles Foster (Journeyman/ Pluto Press, 1993).

Guide to Book Production Practice (British Federation of Master Printers).

Guide to Literary Prizes, Grants and Awards (Compiled by Book Trust and the Society of Authors).

Guide to Self Publishing, Harry Mulholland (Mulholland/Wirral, 1984).

How to Do Your Own Advertising, Michael Bennie (How To Books, 2nd edition).

How to Do Your Own PR, Ian Phillipson (How To Books).

How to Start a Business from Home, Graham Jones (How To Books, 3rd edition).

Inside Book Publishing, Giles Clark (Blueprint, 2nd edition 1994).

Introduction to Desktop Publishing, David Hewson (John Taylor Book Ventures, 1988).

Introduction to Printing Technology (British Printing Industries Federation, price £50).

The Letraset Catalogue, for a comprehensive guide to display typefaces.

The Making of Books, S. Jennet (Faber and Faber).

Managing Your Business Accounts, Peter Taylor (How To Books, 4th edition 1998).

Marketing for Small Publishers, Bill Godber, Robert Webb and Keith Smith (Journeyman/Pluto Press, 2nd edition 1992).

Print — How You Can Do It Yourself, Jonathan Zeitlyn (Interchange Books, 15 Wilkin St, London NW5 3NG).

Publishers in the United Kingdom and Their Addresses (Whitaker).

Publishing Now, Peter Owen (ed.) (Peter Owen, 1993). Up-to-date survey of publishing industry in Britain and USA.

Small Business Guide, Sara Williams (Lloyds Bank).

The Truth about Publishing, S. and P. Unwin (George Allen & Unwin).

UK Book and Learned Journals Printers 1992 (British Printing Industries Federation). List of printers and facilities they offer. Free.

UK Publishers Directory, Ellen Rocco (ed.) (Gale Research International, 1993).

The VAT Guide (HM Customs and Excise, London).

Willings Press Guide (British Media Publications, Windsor Court, East Grinstead House, East Grinstead, West Sussex RH19 1XE, annual).

Writers' and Artists' Yearbook (A & C Black, annual).

The Writer's Handbook, edited by Barry Turner (Macmillan/PEN, annual).

Writing for Publication, Chriss McCallum (How To Books, 4th edition, 1997).

Writing on Disk, Jane Dorner (John Taylor Book Ventures, 1992).

Your Rights:The Liberty Guide, John Wadham (Pluto Press, 1994).

Many of the above books can be obtained from **Book Publishing Books** (BPB), a division of The Publishing Training Centre. Write for an up-to-date catalogue to BPB Administrator, Book Publishing Books, 45 East Hill, Wandsworth, London SW18 2QZ. Tel: (0181) 874 2718; Fax: (0181) 870 8985.

Useful Addresses

American Booksellers Association
828 South Broadway
Tarytown
New York 10591
USA
Tel: (914) 591 2665

Arts Council of Great Britain
105 Piccadilly
London W1V 0AU
Tel: (0171) 629 9495
For information about grants and awards. The Council also publishes a useful (priced) list of press contacts.

(James) Askew and Son Limited
218-222 North Road
Preston PR12 1SY
Tel: (01772) 555947
One of the leading library supply companies.

Association of Little Presses
89A Petterton Road
London N5 2QT
Tel: (0171) 226 2657

Barcodes Ltd
Vale Road
Portslade
East Sussex BN41 1GD
Tel: (01273) 422693
Commercial supplier of barcodes.

Bibliographical Services
J Whitaker and Sons Ltd
12 Dyott Street
London WC1A 1DF
Tel: (08911) 32100

(B.H.) Blackwell Ltd
  Hythe Bridge Street
  Oxford OX1 2ET
  Tel: (01865) 792792
  A leading chain of booksellers and library suppliers.

Book Club Associates
  Smith/Doubleday House
  87 Newman St
  London W1P 3LD
  Tel: (0171) 637 0341

Book Data
  Northumberland House
  2 King Street
  Twickenham TW1 3R2
  Tel: (0181) 892 2272
  Marketing services company, which collects information about new books
  and compiles a database.

Book Marketing Ltd
  7A Bedford Square
  London WC1B 3RA
  Tel: (0171) 580 7282
  Fax: (0171) 580 7236

(The) Bookseller
  J Whitaker and Sons Ltd
  12 Dyott Street
  London WC1A 1DF
  Tel: (08911) 32100
  The leading weekly trade magazine for bookselling and publishing.

(The) Booksellers Association
  272 Vauxhall Bridge Road
  London SW1V 1BB
  Tel: (0171) 834 5477
  Fax: (0171) 834 8812
  The booksellers' trade association from which a directory of members and
  mailing lists can be obtained.

British Amateur Press Association
  78 Tennyson Road
  Stratford
  London E15 4DR

British Association of Picture Libraries & Agencies (BAPLA)
  13 Woodberry Crescent
  London N10 1PJ
  Tel: (0181) 883 2531

An association representing more than 200 picture libraries and picture agencies which hire out their illustrations for a fee.

British Council
Book Promotion Dept
65 Davies Street
London W1Y 2AA
Tel: (0171) 930 8466

British Printing Industries Federation
11 Bedford Row
London WC1R 4DX
Tel: (0171) 242 6904
Fax: (0171) 405 7784

British Standards Institution
2 Park Street
London W1A 2BS
Tel: (0171) 629 9000

Browns Books
P.T. Little and Sons Ltd
22-28 George Street
Kingston-upon-Hull HU1 3AP
Tel: (01482) 25413
Firm of library suppliers.

Chartered Society of Designers
29 Bedford Square
London WC1B 3EG
Tel: (0171) 631 1510

Christian Book Promotion Trust
The Market House
Cantelupe Road
East Grinstead
West Sussex RH19 3BH
Tel: (01342) 312750

Christian Booksellers Association
Grampian House
144 Deansgate
Manchester M3 3ED
Tel: (0161) 833 2848
Fax: (0161) 835 3000

Copyright Licensing Agency Ltd
90 Tottenham Court Road
London W1P 9HE
Tel: (0171) 436 5931
Fax: (0171) 436 3986

HMSO Publications Centre
    PO Box 276
    London SW8 5DT
    Tel: (0171) 622 3316

(The) Holt Jackson Book Company Limited
    Preston Road
    Lytham
    Lancashire FY8 5AX
    Tel: (01253) 737464
    A leading firm of library suppliers.

Independent Publishers Guild
    25 Cambridge Road
    Hampton
    Middlesex TW12 2JL
    Tel/Fax: (0181) 979 0250
    An alternative to the much grander (and more expensive) Publishers
    Association, a useful forum for smaller (and some not-so-small) publishers,
    with a newsletter and national/regional meetings.

ISSN Agency
    ISSN UK Centre
    The British Library
    Boston Spa
    Wetherby
    West Yorkshire LS23 7BY
    Tel: (01937) 546958/9
    Fax: (01937) 546979

Legal Deposit Office
    The British Library
    Boston Spa
    Wetherby
    West Yorkshire LS23 7BY
    Tel: (01937) 546612

Library Association
    7 Ridgmount St
    London
    WC1E 7AB
    Tel: (0171) 636 7543
    Fax: (0171) 636 7218
    The professional organisation for librarians. For a reasonable charge they can
    supply mailing lists of UK libraries, for example on peel-off labels.

Mail Users Association Ltd
  The Wye Valley Business Park
  Brecon Road
  Hay-on-Wye
  Hereford HR3 5PG
  Tel: (01497) 821357
  Fax: (01497) 821360

(The) Morley Book Co Ltd
  Elmfield Road
  Morley
  Leeds
  LS27 0NN
  Tel: (0113) 201 2900
  A leading firm of library suppliers.

Public Lending Right Office
  Bayheath House
  Prince Regent Street
  Stockton-on-Tees
  Cleveland TS18 1DF
  Tel: (01642) 604699

Publishers Association
  19 Bedford Square
  London WC1B 3HJ
  Tel: (0171) 580 6321-5
  Fax: (0171) 636 5375

Publishers Publicity Circle
  Christina Thomas (Secretary)
  48 Crabtree Lane
  London SW6 6LW
  Tel/Fax: (0171) 385 3708

Publishing News
  43 Museum Street
  London
  WC1A 1LY
  Tel: (0171) 404 0304
  Fax: (0171) 242 0762

(The) Publishing Training Centre at Book House
    45 East Hill
    Wandsworth
    London SW18 2QZ
    Tel: (0181) 874 2718
    Fax: (0181) 870 8985
    E-mail:publishing.training@bookhouse.co.uk

Scottish Publishers Association
    Scottish Book Centre
    137 Dundee Street
    Edinburgh EH11 1BG
    Tel: (0131) 228 6866
    Fax: (0131) 228 3220

(Mr A. T.) Smail
    Agent for the Copyright Libraries
    100 Euston St
    London NW1 2HQ
    Tel: (0171) 388 5061

Small Press Group of Britain
    Small Press Centre
    Middlesex University
    White Hart Lane
    London N17
    Tel: (0181) 362 6058

Society of Authors
    84 Drayton Gardens
    London SW10 9SD
    Tel: (0171) 373 6642

Society of Freelance Editors and Proofreaders
    1 Mermaid Court
    London SE1 1HR
    Tel: (0171) 403 4947

Society of Indexers
    Mermaid House
    1 Mermaid Court
    London SE1 1HR
    Tel: (0171) 403 4947

Society of Picture Researchers and Editors
    BM Box 259
    London WC1N 3XX
    Tel: (0171) 404 5011

Standard Book Numbering Agency Ltd
    12 Dyott Street
    London WC1A 1DF
    Tel: (08911) 32100

Teleordering Ltd
    Wellington House
    61-73 Staines Road West
    Sunbury-on-Thames
    Middlesex TW16 7AH
    Tel: (01392) 781266

Union of Welsh Publishers and Booksellers
    (Undeb Cyhoeddwyr a Llyfrwerthwyr Cymraeg)
    c/o Gomer Press
    Llandysul
    Dyfed SA44 4BQ
    Tel: (01559) 362371
    Fax: (01559) 363758

(J) Whitaker and Sons Ltd
    12 Dyott Street
    London WC1A 1DF
    Tel: (08911) 32100
    Fax: (0171) 836 4342

    Also *The Bookseller*; *Books in Print*; Society of Young Publishers, Standard Address Numbering Agency; Standard Book Numbering Agency; Users of Book Industry Standards.

Women in Publishing
    c/o 12 Dyott Street
    London WC1A 1DF
    Tel: (08911) 32100

Writers' Guild of Great Britain
    430 Edgware Road
    London W2 1EH
    Tel: (0171) 723 8074
    Fax: (0171) 706 2413

Appendix 1
UK Colleges, Universities and Other Institutions Offering Publishing Courses

If you would like to explore publishing in greater depth, perhaps with a view to a career in publishing, here is a list of institutions offering courses/qualifications:

The Publishing Training Centre at Book House
45 East Hill
Wandsworth
London
SW18 2QZ
Tel: (0181) 874 2718
Fax: (0181) 870 8985
E-mail: publishing.training.@bookhouse.co.uk

Offers a comprehensive range of short courses in publishing and management skills. The majority of courses are non-residential and are held at Book House in Wandsworth. Courses include 'Book Publishing, an Introduction'; 'Copy-Editing Skills'; 'Book Production for Editors'; 'Copyright and Contracts'; 'Foundation Course in Book Production'; 'Making Marketing Work in Book Publishing'; 'Promotion and PR'.

London College of Printing and Distributive Trades
School of Printing Technology
Elephant & Castle, London SE1 6SB
Tel: (0171) 735 8484

(1) Diploma in Printing and Publishing Studies for Graduates — 17 weeks.
(2) Diploma in Publishing Production — 35 weeks.
Contacts: Dr A. K. Maitra; Steve McFarlane.

Department of Information and Library Studies
Loughborough University
Loughborough LE11 3TU
Tel: (01509) 223050
Fax: (01509) 223053

MA in Publishing — one year.
Contact: Professor J. P. Feather.

Middlesex University
Queensway, Enfield
Middx EN3 4SF
Tel: (0181) 368 1299
Fax: (0181) 805 0702

(1) BA in Writing and Publishing — 3 years.
(2) MA in Computer Integrated Publishing — 1 year.
Contact: Dr Clive Bloom.

Napier Polytechnic of Edinburgh
Colinton Road
Edinburgh EH10 5QT
Tel: (0131) 444 2266
Fax: (0131) 452 8532

BA Publishing — 3 years.
Contact: Dr Sheila Lodge.

Oxford Brookes University
Gipsy Lane
Oxford OX3 0BP
Tel: (01865) 741111
Fax: (01865) 819073

(1) BA/BSc (publishing and another subject) — 3 years.
(2) Diploma in Advanced Studies in Publishing — 1 year.
Contact: Kelvin Smith.

The Robert Gordon Institute of Technology
School of Librarianship and Information Studies
Hilton Place
Aberdeen AB9 1FP
Tel: (01224) 283835
Fax: (01224) 488545

BA(Hons) in Publishing Studies — 3 years.
Contact: Priscilla Schlicke.

Thames Valley University
St Mary's Road, Ealing W5 5RF
Tel: (0181) 579 5000
Fax: (0181) 566 1353

Information Management (Publishing) — BA(Hons) — 3 years.
Contact: Michael Strain.

University of Plymouth
Faculty of Arts and Design
Earl Richards Road North
Exeter EX2 6AS
Tel: (01392) 412211
Fax: (01392) 475012

(1) MA — 48 weeks.
(2) Postgraduate Diploma in Publishing and Book Production — 24 weeks.
Contact: Paul Honeywill.

Centre for Publishing Studies
University of Stirling
Stirling FK9 4LA
Tel: (01786) 73171
Fax: (01786) 51335

Publishing Studies — MPhil or Postgraduate Diploma — 1 year.
Contact: Dr Ian McGowan.

West Herts College
Hempstead Road,
Watford WD1 3EZ
Tel: (01923) 257660/1
Fax: (01992) 257556

(1) BSc (Hons) in Graphic Media Studies — 4 years.
(2) Diploma in Publishing — 6 months.
Contacts: Wendy Tury; Ivor Powell.

Appendix 2
Checklists of Tasks

Set out below are checklists of tasks and skills in a number of areas of book publishing. They are drawn from the *Skill Audits* issued by the Publishing Training Centre at Book House (see Appendix 1) as part of the process of setting standards for assessment and training in the publishing industry.

I suggest that you use the checklists as a means of clarifying the different tasks you will need to accomplish to publish *your* book. They should also help you to identify the skills and abilities you already have, and where you might need to seek further advice, assistance or training.

Book commissioning

Identify and assess publishing market:
- identify and assess current and future market trends and opportunities
- plan and use market research techniques.

Develop a publishing strategy:
- taking into account financial resources, production know-how and selling capability.

Develop individual publishing projects:
- taking into account market factors, profit targets and financial and other resources.

Process projects:
- vet content for legal and other checks (see under editing below)
  - libel
  - defamation
  - blasphemy
  - obscenity
  - stereotyping

  - sexism
  - culture bias
  - related forms of discrimination
- ensure editing of projects (see below)
- provide production briefs and monitor progress
  - artwork and illustrations
  - indexes
  - typographical treatment
  - formal, page size, extent
  - paper quality
  - binding and finishing.

Book editing

Edit text:
- ensure factual accuracy and consistency for names, dates, events, people, places etc
- ensure structural correctness and consistency of style for
  - spelling, grammar, punctuation, capitalisation, hyphenation
  - representation of numbers and dates
  - units of measurement
  - abbreviations and contractions
  - cross-referencing
  - logical sequencing of text
  - notes and references
- mark up text for typesetting, dealing with
  - hierarchy of headings
  - paragraphing
  - textual references to notes, footnotes, glossaries and bibliographies
  - any parts of text requiring special typographical treatment
- prepare and mark up preliminary pages
  - title, author, editor(s), translator(s), publisher
  - dedication
  - foreword and preface
  - contents list, list of illustrations, etc
  - copyright page: publisher, copyright protection, ISBN, CIP, printer
- ensure text conforms to legal requirements
  - libel
  - blasphemy

- plagiarism
- passing off
- offence to national or religious groups.

Proof read and collate text:
- read and correct text proofs
  - fidelity to typescript or previous stage of proof
  - implementation of corrections in previous stage of proof
  - saving and making lines
  - internal consistency and accuracy of spelling and book style
  - typographical alterations including layout, heading weights, indents, turnover lines, spacing and font
  - running heads
  - contents list
  - page numbers
- collate alterations to text proofs when text has been read by more than one person (eg author, editor, publisher, freelance proof reader).

Check, edit and mark up index, ensuring consistency with text for spelling, hyphenation, capitalisation etc.

Book design
Design factors to consider include:
- format
- type of paper
- number of pages
- colour printing
- typography
- binding style
- illustrations and their integration into the text
- use of tints and colour
- legibility and aesthetic appeal.

Book production
Prepare production specifications, covering:
- page size
- extent
- quality and weight of paper
- print run
- ink colours
- number and type of illustrations

- binding style
- covers, jackets and printed paper cases
- packing and delivery requirements.

Operate within planned purchasing policy, budgets and schedules, taking into account:
- terms of trade for payment and invoicing
- credit terms and arrangements
- competitiveness of quotes (price, quality of work, capacity, delivery dates, past performance etc).

Record production costs.

Control the quality throughout the production process:
- check printing for quality and evenness of inking; position and alignment of pages; text and cover
- check paper for quality, quantity and size
- check binding for strength, durability, trimming and finish.

Publicity and promotion

Identify publicity and promotion objectives.

Select appropriate publicity and promotion strategies, taking into account:
- promotional budget
- overall marketing plan
- book production schedules
- projected sales targets
- deadlines.

Prepare promotional materials and organise advertising:
- advertising copy to identify
  - key features of product
  - benefits
  - publisher
  - author
  - publication date.

Create and exploit publicity opportunities:
- publicity strategy to be influenced by

- author's publicity profile
- contents and topicality of title
- unique selling points
- personal media contacts
● publicity campaign strategies to be considered and evaluated include
  - author-based promotion including press, radio and TV interviews, conferences, lectures and demonstrations
  - competitions, editorial mentions and book shop promotions.

Create and maintain media contacts.

Monitor and evaluate publicity activities.

Plan and execute direct mail campaigns:

● develop, manage and maintain mailing lists, derived from
  - past purchasers
  - mailing and prospect lists
  - exhibition attendees
  - market response devices
  - directories
  - societies and associations
  - subscribers to relevant journals, list exchanges etc
● establish direct mail systems for customer payment options and order returns
● ensure systems cover
  - address labels
  - letters, inserts and other promotional materials
  - files and other records
  - packaging
  - delivery
● monitor and evaluate direct mail campaigns.

Organise publicity and promotion input to sales conferences and exhibitions.

Index